Ephraim Kirby, Court Connecticut. Superior, Superior Court Connecticut

Reports of cases adjudged in the Superior Court of the State of Connecticut : from the year 1785 to May 1788

With some determinations in the Supreme Court of Errors

Ephraim Kirby, Court Connecticut. Superior, Superior Court Connecticut

Reports of cases adjudged in the Superior Court of the State of Connecticut : from the year 1785 to May 1788
With some determinations in the Supreme Court of Errors

ISBN/EAN: 9783337184902

Printed in Europe, USA, Canada, Australia, Japan

Cover: Foto ©Suzi / pixelio.de

More available books at **www.hansebooks.com**

REPORTS

OF

CASES

ADJUDGED IN THE

SUPERIOR COURT

OF THE

State of Connecticut.

FROM THE YEAR 1785, TO MAY 1788;

WITH SOME

DÉTERMINATIONS

IN THE

SUPREME COURT OF ERRORS.

BY EPHRAIM KIRBY, ESQUIRE.

LITCHFIELD: PRINTED BY COLLIER & ADAM.

M,DCC,LXXXIX.

PREFACE.

THE uncertainty and contradiction attending the judicial decisions in this state, have long been subjects of complaint.—The source of this complaint is easily discovered.—When our ancestors emigrated here, they brought with them the notions of jurisprudence which prevailed in the country from whence they came.—The riches, luxury, and extensive commerce of that country, contrasted with the equal distribution of property, simplicity of manners, and agricultural habits and employments of this, rendered a deviation from the English laws, in many instances, highly necessary. This was observed—and the intricate and prolix practice of the English courts was rejected, and a mode of practice more simple, and better accommodated to an easy and speedy administration of justice, adopted.——Our courts were still in a state of embarrassment, sensible that the common law of England, " though a highly improved system," was not fully applicable to our situation ; but no provision being made to preserve and publish proper histories of their adjudications, every attempt of the Judges, to run the line of distinction, between what was applicable and what not, proved abortive : For the principles of their decisions were soon forgot, or misunderstood, or erroneously reported from memory.—Hence arose a confusion in the determinations of our courts ;—the rules of property became uncertain, and litigation proportionably encreased.

In this situation, some legislative exertion was found necessary ; and in the year 1785 an act passed, requiring the Judges of the Superior Court, to render written reasons for their decisions, in cases where the pleadings closed in an issue at law.—This was a great advance toward improvement ; still it left the business of reformation but half performed :— For the arguments of the Judges, without a history of the whole case, would not always be intelligible ; and they would

become

become known to but few perfons ; and being written on loofe papers, were expofed to be miflaid, and foon fink into total oblivion.—Befides, very many important matters are determined on motions of various kinds, where no written reafons are rendered, and fo are liable to be forever loft.

Hence it became obvious to every one, that fhould hiftories of important caufes be carefully taken and publifhed, in which the whole procefs fhould appear, fhowing the true grounds and principles of the decifion, it would produce a permanent fyftem of common law.—But the court being ambulatory through the ftate, the undertaking would be attended with confiderable expence and interruption of other bufinefs, without any profpect of private advantage; therefore, no gentleman of the profeffion feemed willing to make fo great a facrifice.—I had entered upon this bufinefs in a partial manner, for private ufe ; which came to the knowledge of feveral gentlemen of diftinction.—I was urged to purfue it more extenfively ;—and being perfuaded that an attempt of the kind (however imperfect) might be made in fome degree fubfervient to the great object, I compiled the Volume of Reports which is now prefented to the public,—Could any effort of mine induce government to provide for the profecution of fo neceffary a work by a more able hand, my wifhes would be gratified, and my labour, in accomplifhing this, amply repaid.

In thefe Reports, I have endeavoured to throw the matter into as fmall a compafs as was confiftent with a right underftanding of the cafe:—Therefore, I have not ftated the pleadings or arguments of counfel further than was neceffary to bring up the points relied on; except fome few inftances which feemed to require a more lengthy detail of argument.—As the work is defigned for general ufe in this ftate, I have avoided technical terms and phrafes as much as poffible, that it might be intelligible to all claffes of men.—Some cafes are reported which are merely local, and have reference to the peculiar practice of this ftate ; thefe may appear unimportant to readers in other ftates ; but they were neceffary to the great object of the work.

I am

I am sensible that this production is introduced to the world under circumstances very unfavourable to its reputation.—But however diffident I might be, under other circumstances, I feel an honest confidence in this attempt to advance the common interest of my fellow-citizens ;—and that, so obvious are the difficulties which must occur in almost every stage of the business, that to detail them in a preface would be offering an insult to the understanding of my readers.— The candid and generous, if they read these Reports, will doubtless find frequent occasion to draw into exercise those excellent virtues ; and as to readers of an opposite disposition, I have neither wishes or fears concerning them.—If any one should experience disagreeable sensations, from the inelegance of this performance, let him rest assured he cannot more sincerely regret its faults than I do.

―――――――――――――――――――――――――

HAVING perused Mr. KIRBY's " Reports of " Cases adjudged in the Superior Court, from " the Year 1785 to May, 1788," it appears to us that the Cases are truly reported.

RICHARD LAW,
ELIPHALET DYER,
ROGER SHERMAN,
WILLIAM PITKIN,
OLIVER ELLSWORTH.

―――――――――――――――――――――――――

An

ALPHABETICAL TABLE

OF THE

NAMES OF THE CASES.

NAMES OF THE CASES.

ARGUED AND DETERMINED

IN THE

SUPERIOR COURT

OF THE

STATE OF CONNECTICUT.

COUNTY *of* LITCHFIELD, *Feb. Term*, 1786.

RICHARD LAW, *Efq. Chief Juftice,*
ELIPHALET DYER, *Efq.*
ROGER SHERMAN, *Efq.*
WILLIAM PITKIN, *Efq.*
OLIVER ELLSWORTH, *Efq.*
} *Judges.*

WHITING *and* FRISBIE *againft* JEWEL.

IN this cafe depofitions were offered by the defendant, which were taken in the commonwealth of Maffachufetts, more than twenty miles diftant from the plaintiffs' refidence, but within ten miles of their known agent and attorney, neither of them being notified or prefent at the caption.

It was objected, that thefe depofitions were not fo taken as to come within the fpirit of the ftatute allowing affidavits to be made out of court;—which is, that, " Forafmuch as it is " neceffary that witneffes in civil caufes be " fworn out of court, when by reafon of their " going to fea, living more than twenty miles " diftant

[marginal note:] When depofitions are taken out of this ftate, notice fhould be given to the adverfe party, or to his known agent or attorney, if within 20 miles of the caption, and if the party himfelf lives out of this ftate, & have a known attorney or agent in the ftate, he fhall be notified.

1786.

Whiting
and
Frisbie
against
Jewel.

" distant from the place where the cause is to
" be tried, age, sickness or bodily infirmity,
" they are rendered incapable of travel, and of
" appearing at court.——To the intent, there-
" fore, that all witnesses may impartially and
" indifferently testify their certain knowledge,
" and the whole truth in the cause they are to
" speak to; therefore,

" *Be it enacted,* &c.——That for either of the
" reasons aforesaid, and not otherwise, every
" Assistant or Justice of the Peace, may take
" affidavits out of court; so as a notification,
" with reasonable time, be first made out and
" delivered to the adverse party, (if within
" twenty miles of the place) or left at the place
" of his dwelling, or usual abode, to be present
" at the time of taking such affidavit, if he
" think fit."

BY THE COURT.——In taking depositions
within this state, the statute requires notice to
the adverse party, if within twenty miles: As
to those taken out of the state, which the statute
in strictness does not extend to, and which can
only be admitted on the ground of their being
so taken as to come fully within the equity of the
statute; there ought to be notice to the adverse
party or to his known agent or attorney, if either are within twenty miles of the place of
caption; which not having been given in this
case the deposition is not admissible.

Judge SHERMAN, *dissenting.*——The adverse
party in this case lived more than twenty miles
from the place of caption, and the statute does
not in any case require notice to be given to an
agent or attorney.

HORSFORD and AGARD against WRIGHT.

Action on the covenant of seisin in a deed of bargain and sale.

By LAW, Chief Justice.

IN actions on the covenant of warranty, the constant rule of this court, has been, to assertain damages, by the value of the land, at the time of eviction, though the *British* rule is to give the confideration of the deed.—The diversity in this respect, between the *British* practice and ours, is undoubtedly founded in the permanent worth of their lands, as an old country, and the increasing worth of ours, as a new country. —And it is supposed that the purchaser goes on, improves and makes the land better till he is evicted.—But query, whether this reasoning will apply to an action brought on the covenant of seisin; for in that case the purchaser does not wait till he is evicted, but brings his action immediately upon discovery that his title is defective; and it is presumed he will immediately acquaint himself with the strength of his title.

The jury computed the damages by the latter rule, and returned a verdict which was accepted by the whole court.

In an action on the covenant of seisin, contained in a deed of bargain & sale, the rule of damages is the confideration of the deed; but on the covenant of warranty, the value of the land at the time of eviction.

MILLS *against* BISHOP *and* WETMORE.

If several de-
fendants are
described in
the procefs
as being in-
habitants of
this ftate,
there muft be
fervice on
all, though
fome of them
at the time of
fervice may
not be within
the ftate;

THIS was an attachment in which both defendants were defcribed as inhabitants of
the town of Litchfield. The officer made return that he had attached the eftate of *John
Bifhop,* one of the defendants, and had left with
him a true and attefted copy of the writ, &c.
and that the other defendant was out of the ftate.

The defendants, pleaded in abatement, that
the writ had never been legally ferved, for, by
the officer's return, no fervice had been made
upon *Wetmore,* one of the defendants.

The plaintiff replied, that the defendant,
Wetmore, after the date of the writ, and before
the fervice, removed out of this ftate into Nova-
Scotia, a province in America, fubject to the
king of Great-Britain; therefore, the law required no fervice to be made on him, but that
fervice on the other defendant was fufficient to
fupport the procefs.

The defendants demurred fpecially, and for
caufe alledged, that the plaintiff, having in her
writ defcribed both of the defendants as inhabitants of the town of Litchfield, fhe is therefore
eftopped from pleading any new matter, repugnant to that defcription.

Mr. *Tracy* and Mr. *Kirby,* for the defendants,
contended that the officer was bound ftrictly to
purfue the direction given in his precept;—
which was, to make fervice on each of the defendants, by attaching their perfons, or eftate,
and leaving attefted copies with each of them,
or at their laft ufual place of abode within this
ftate.—The ftatute referred to in the replication,
is, " That in actions on joint fecurities, or con-
" tracts,

1786.

Mills
againſt
Biſhop
and
Wetmore.

" tracts, where all the defendants are not inhabi-
" tants of this ſtate, the ſervice of the proceſs
" on ſuch of the defendants as are inhabitants
" of this ſtate (if any) ſhall be ſufficient notice
" to maintain the ſuit againſt all the defendants.
" And if any ſuch defendant on whom the pro-
" ceſs was not ſerved is aggrieved, by the judg-
" ment, he may be relieved by *audita querela*."
—This ſtatute does not extend to any ſuit where
the defendants are not in the writ deſcribed as
belonging out of this ſtate, and an oppoſite
conſtruction would introduce inconſiſtency into
the record.

Mr. *Canfield* and Mr. *Reeve*, for the plaintiff,
urged that it appeared from the pleadings, the
defendant, *Wetmore*, who had not been ſerved
with the proceſs, was not an inhabitant of this
ſtate at the time of ſervice; therefore this caſe
is clearly within the reaſon of the ſtatute.—That
under ſuch circumſtances, it avails nothing to
leave a copy at the laſt uſual place of abode,
becauſe notice of the ſuit is not obtained by it—
That theſe matters coming up in the courſe of
the pleadings, places it on the ſame footing as
if expreſſed in the body of the declaration, becauſe it becomes equally a part of the record,
and makes the whole proceſs conſiſtent.

The replication adjudged inſufficient—and
that the proceſs abate.

On motion, the plaintiff was allowed to
amend the deſcriptive part of her writ, paying
coſt.——And

By the Court——Motion for amend-
ment is unneceſſary: For the ſtatute, which
enacts, " That when any plea ſhall be made in
" abatement of any writ or proceſs, before the
" ſuperior or county court, or before any Aſ-
" ſiſtant or Juſtice of the Peace, that if it be
" ruled

Mills
against
Bifhop
and
Wetmore.

", ruled in favour of the defendant, the plaintiff
" fhall have liberty to amend that defect, his
" paying down to the defendant his cofts to
" that time; and then to proceed as he might
" have done if no fuch defect had been;" al-
lows the plaintiff always to amend his writ on
paying coft: And if he doth not cure the defect
by amendment, the defendant may again plead
in abatement.

LAWRENCE *against* KINGMAN.

The certifi-
cate of a Juf-
tice who if-
fues a writ
directed to an
indifferent
perfon to
ferve, becaufe
no proper of-
ficer can be
had without
great expenfe
and inconve-
nience, is
conclufive;
and the court
will not en-
quire, as to
the truth of
fuch certifi-
cate.

THE writ was directed to an indifferent perfon to ferve and return, and the authority
figning it had inferted the common reafon, 'that
no proper officer could be had without great
expence." The defendant pleaded in abatement, that the writ was dated a fufficient length
of time before the time of fervice expired, to
have been ferved by a proper officer, with the
ordinary expence only; and therefore the certificate of the Juftice was manifeftly a miftake.

BY THE COURT——The certificate of the
figning authority is conclufive, and the Court
will never enquire into the truth of fuch certificate.* This point has been frequently adjudged.

---

* The ftatute which empowers the figning authority to
direct a writ to an indifferent perfon, is as follows—" And
" all writs and proceffes fhall be directed to the Sheriff,
" his deputy, or fome conftable, if no officer can be had
" without great charge or inconvenience: And in every
" cafe wherein the authority figning a writ fhall find it ne-
" ceffary to direct the fame to an indifferent perfon, fuch
" authority fhall infert the name of fuch indifferent perfon
" in the direction of the writ, and the reafon of fuch di-
" rection; and if any writ be otherwife directed it fhall
" abate."

judged. The last *term* the case of *Allen* vs. *Jones* came up by appeal on pleas of abatement—It was the same question; and the Court then expressed their surprise that the lower courts were unacquainted with this point in practice, which had been so fully settled.

The writ established.

PAGE, *against* CAMP.

Error from the judgement of a Justice of the Peace.

CAMP, the defendant in error, brought his action against *Page*, the plaintiff in error, before Justice *O. P.* stating in his declaration, "That said *Page* commenced an action of "Book-debt against him before Justice *D. W.* "demanding forty shillings, &c.—to which he "pleaded that he owed nothing.—And on trial "of said cause, the only articles exhibited by "said *Page* as his charge on book, were sundry "casks, (to wit) hogsheads, butts and barrels; "which he testified, had been by him delivered "to the care of said *Camp* some time before, "and that they were then good and valuable, "and that he (said *Page*) had never seen or "heard of them after the delivery.—By means "of which testimony and information given by "said *Page* on said trial, he recovered of said "*Camp* by the judgement of said Justice *W.* "twenty-nine shillings debt and eighteen shil-"lings cost.—That the testimony and informa-"tion of said *Page* to said Justice, respecting "said casks, was false; for said casks, at the "time of said pretended delivery, were all un-"found

An action for perjury is not sustainable before a Justice of Peace, unless the defendant has been previously convicted; neither can new trials be granted by a single Minister of Law; or the decision of one, be subjected to the re examination or impeachment of another.

" found and of very little value ; and that said
" Page, after the time of said pretended deli-
" very, had taken them all out of the cuftody
" of said Camp and difpofed of them;—which
" facts did not appear on trial, becaufe they
" were then unknown to faid Camp : And by
" reafon of which falfe information given by
" faid Page in the premifes, faid Camp is dam-
" nified, &c.

On a demurrer to this declaration, judgement was rendered for the plaintiff.

Mr. *Tracy* and Mr. *Kirby*, for the plaintiff in
error, took two exceptions to this judgement—
1ft, That the action was not fuftainable, being
brought to draw again into controverfy, facts
which had once been adjudged by a court of
competent and final jurifdiction.——2nd, That
the declaration fuppofes a fraud in the defendant, but contains no allegation of fcience, without which no action for fraud is fuftainable.

Mr. *Adams* and Mr. *Reeve*, in fupport of the
judgement, contended, that this action did not
call in queftion the former judgement rendered
by Juftice *W.* but is in nature of an *indebitatus
affumpfit* to recover back money obtained by
fraud.—The facts alledged in the declaration
amount to a charge of perjury, and therefore
contain the higheft poffible charge of fraud.—
They relied principally on the cafe of *Mofes* and
Macfarlan, 2 *Burrow* 1005.

Judgement reverfed.

By THE COURT——An action for perjury is
not fuftainable by a fingle Minifter of Law, unlefs for damages confequent upon conviction;
and there is no averment in the declaration,
of *fcience* in the party who teftified, that his teftimony was falfe, without which it could not be
perjury.—But the action was brought againft a
party to a former fuit for fupporting facts by his
own

own teftimony, which it is averred would be found un~~~~ upon new evidence.——This would have been a ground for a new trial, had the cafe been of fufficient magnitude : But the law doth not admit of new trials before a Juftice of the Peace, nor doth it fubject the decifions of one Juftice of the Peace to the re-examination or impeachment of another, to which, an affirmance of the judgement in this cafe would be giving countenance.

The authority of *Macfarlan's* cafe, cited and relied on in fupport of the judgement, does not apply ; the cafes materially differ.—*Indebitatus affumpfit* was there maintained for money recovered before a Court of confcience ; but maintained on grounds of which the Court of confcience had no cognizance, and to which their decifion had no relation.—In this cafe, one Juftice re-examines the truth of facts, over the head of another Juftice, of fimilar jurifdiction, and, in fact, tries the fame cafe, a fecond time.

DYER and PITKIN, *Judges, diffenting.*—In this cafe there is a fraud alledged of the higheft kind—a taking of property by wilful falfe fwearing in a Court of Juftice.—Why, then, fhould there not be a remedy, and why is not this a proper one ?—The reafon, that the public will fuftain an inconvenience by fuch a practice, does not counterbalance the injury that will be fuftained by leaving fuch injuftice remedylefs ; therefore, the fuit ought to be fupported on principles of public policy as well as public juftice.—The objection that there is not enough alledged in the declaration, is not a folid one. We rarely alledge more in any declaration for fraud. The facts ftated are fuch, that the fcience and intention of the defendant muft follow as a neceffary and unavoidable conclufion.

It is faid if this action prevails, it will eftab-

B   lifh

Page
against
Camp.

lish a principle, by which one Juftice will interfere with the decifions of another. That
confequence will not follow. The firft Juftice
was undoubtedly right, and decided upon good
reafons: The fecond may adjudge in favour of
the oppofite party, and be equally right; for
the queftion before the laft is a very different
one from the former.—Here is no interference
of jurifdiction—no clafhing of judgements.—
This action is well fupported by the general
principles of common law.—It is a ftrong cafe;
for it is agreed there is no remedy for the injury complained of, unlefs the prefent action be
fupported: Therefore we cannot fay the judgement is erroneous.

HINMAN *and others, Adminiftrators of* HINMAN
againft STILES.

ACTION of book-debt, *nil debet* pleaded,
and verdict for the plaintiff.———The
defendant moved in arreft of judgement; and
for caufe alledged, that the account produced on trial, contained a charge of about forty
pounds for a tract of land, and alfo a charge
of about three pounds as intereft on part of the
account; both of which were illegal as charges
on book, and both were allowed by the jury,
in their verdict.†

Motion over-ruled.

By

---

† N. B. It is the cuftom of the courts in the ftate of
Connecticut, to admit motions in arreft, which are conver-
fant about facts, dehors the record: And likewife, by the
cuftom of courts, the adverfe party is not obliged to make
any anfwer either by way of traverfe or demurrer; but the
court proceed to enquire the truth of fuch facts, unlefs the
oppofite party choofes to demur.

Hinman
and others
againſt
Stiles.

BY THE COURT.——On examination of two of the jurors, it appears that the jury found the ſum of 40*l.* credited to the defendant, which was equal to the ſum charged for the land, and which by agreement of the parties was to be in payment for the land; and that the ſmall ſums of intereſt included in the verdict, were not, on trial, objected to by the defendant: And one witneſs teſtified, that they were charged by conſent of the defendant.——There were other proper book-debt articles in the account, to a large amount, to which there was no objection;—and the balance would have been the ſame, if the land, and ſum credited for it, had not been entered on the book:—Therefore the motion in arreſt is inſufficient.

Judge DYER, *diſſenting.*——He ſaid that the admiſſion of ſuch charges on book, ſupported by the parties' oath, would tend to introduce the greateſt imaginable confuſion.   The nature of the thing rendered the idea of ſuch a charge on book abſurd;—becauſe, when a deed of land is made out, the grantor acknowledges the conſideration to be paid to his full ſatisfaction at the time of the grant; and it is both dangerous and abſurd, that ſo high an evidence ſhould be ſet aſide by the parties' own oath.

NOTT

Nott *against* Welles.

Recognizances for fpecial bail may be taken to the party for whofe benefit they are intended.

ACTION of debt on a recognizance for fpecial bail.—The recognizance was taken to the adverfe party and not to the county treafurer.

On demurrer to the declaration, the only exception was, that the recognizance was improperly taken, for that it ought to have been taken to the county treafurer and not to the adverfe party.

Declaration adjudged fufficient.

By the Court.——The recognizance on which this action is brought was well taken, though before the ftatute directing that in certain cafes recognizances fhall be taken to the adverfe party.——There does not appear any fufficient reafon why bonds of recognizance might not ever have been taken to the perfon for whofe benefit they were intended, as well as other bonds; though a different mode of taking them has been practifed, and may yet alfo be good, in cafes where there is no ftatute direction.

Beers *against* Strong.

Words are not to be taken in the milder fenfe af erverdict, which afcertains him to have been fpoken malicioufly.

ACTION on the cafe for thefe words:——
" My wife has taken a falfe oath, and it
" was through the inftigation of *Beers* and *Booth,*
" her fons.——My wife has taken a falfe oath—
" fhe is a poor creature—and if it had not been
" for *Andrew Beers* and *David Booth,* fhe never
" would have done it;—they are the foundation
" of the quarrel.——My wife's children have
" taken her before 'fquire *Hinman,* and have
" made

" made her take a falſe oath, and I have been
" and taken a copy of it.——*David Booth* and
" *Andrew Beers* took my wife before 'ſquire
" *Hinman*, and there perſuaded her to take a
" falſe oath, and I don't blame her ſo much as
" I do *Booth* and *Beers*, for they were the very
" means of it, and ſhe never would have done
" it but for them.".

General iſſue pleaded, and verdict for the
plaintiff.

Mr. *Edwards* moved in arreſt, on the ground
that the words were not actionable.

Motion over-ruled.

By the Court.——The words laid, natu-
rally import that the defendant's wife had been
guilty of perjury, and that the plaintiff, by
procuring her to commit the crime, had been
guilty of ſubornation of perjury, and ſo are
actionable.——Words are not to be taken in a
milder ſenſe than they have in common accept-
ation; eſpecially after verdict, which aſcertains
that they were ſpoken maliciouſly, and with intent to defame.

———————————

Tweedy *againſt* Brush.

ACTION of trover, general iſſue pleaded,
and verdict for the defendant.——The
plaintiff moved in arreſt; and for cauſe alledged, that two of the jurors who tried ſaid cauſe,
and were in favour of ſaid verdict, before they
were ſworn and impannelled to try the ſame,
had given their opinion in favour of the defendant: And that one of ſaid jurors, after the
cauſe was committed to them for their conſideration, and before they had delivered their
ſaid

*If a juror be-
fore trial has
given his
opinion in a
cauſe, and
this be not
known by
the party,
againſt
whom the
opinion ope-
rates; it is
ſufficient
cauſe for an
arreſt.*

1786.

Tweedy
againſt
Bruſh.

ſaid verdict to the Court, gave and publiſhed his opinion in ſaid cauſe to other perſons, not of the jury, and converſed with them reſpecting ſaid cauſe.

Motion in arreſt ſufficient.

BY THE COURT—*(Judge* SHERMAN *abſent)* On enquiry, it appears, that before the jury were impannelled, two of them had formed and declared opinions in favour of the defendant, which was not known by the plaintiff: Therefore, this caſe has not had a fair and impartial trial.

HOBBY *againſt* FINCH *and* KNAPP.

An adver-
tiſement that
lands are to
be ſold at
public auc-
tion, with
the terms of
the ſale, &c.
is a ſufficient
memoran-
dum in wri-
ting within
the ſtatute of
frauds, to
hold the
vendor to a
performance
of his agree-
ment.

THE declaration ſtates, that the defendants were adminiſtrators on the eſtate of *Caleb Finch*, deceaſed; and had obtained an order from the court of probate to ſell at public vendue a tract of land belonging to ſaid eſtate, and that, by a number of advertiſements, they gave notice of the time and place of ſale.—That the plaintiff attended at the time and place appointed by the defendants in their advertiſements, where the conditions of the ſale of ſaid land were publiſhed and made known to the plaintiff by the defendants;—which were, that the land ſo ſet up for ſale, ſhould be ſtruck off to the higheſt bidder, and a deed ſigned and executed by the defendants to the perſon that ſhould pay to them the greateſt price, or become obligated to them in the largeſt ſum of money, (with ſurety if required) for ſaid land——And that the plaintiff, according to the conditions ſo made known, did bid the higheſt price for ſaid land, and became obligated with ſurety to the defendants in the greateſt ſum of money of any perſon preſent prefent at the time where faid land was offered for fale as aforefaid; but that the defendants have never executed faid deed according to the tenor of their promife, &c.

Mr. *Sturgefs*, for the defendants, pleaded in bar, that the agreement mentioned in the declaration, was never reduced to writing, nor was there any memorandum or note thereof ever made in writing and figned by the defendants, or any other perfon by them thereunto lawfully authorized, which is made neceffary by the ftatute " *for prevention of frauds and perjuries.*"

Mr. *Davenport* and Mr. *Thompfon*, for the plaintiff, replied, particularly defcribing the *advertifements* and *conditions of fale*, figned by the defendants, and that the plaintiff had fully complied with the terms therein expreffed; and that therefore there was a memorandum, or note made in writing, of the agreement mentioned in the declaration.

On demurrer, to the replication, the only queftion was, whether the advertifements and conditions of fale, defcribed in the pleadings, were fuch a memorandum of the agreement as would fave this cafe out of the ftatute of frauds: By which it is enacted,—" That no fuit in law " or equity fhall be brought or maintained upon " any contract, or fale of lands, tenements, or " hereditaments, or any intereft in or concern- " ing them; unlefs the agreement upon which " fuch action fhall be brought, or fome memo- " randum or note thereof fhall be made in wri- " ting, and figned by the party to be charged " therewith, or fome other perfon thereunto by " him lawfully authorized."

Replication adjudged fufficient.

BY THE COURT.——The advertifements and conditions of fale, fet forth in the reply of the plaintiff,

1786.

Hobby
againſt
Finch, &c.

§ 1 Black-
ſtone's Re-
ports 599,
Simon vs.
Metivier.
3. Burr.
1921. S. C.
1. Wilſon,
118.--Wel-
ford vs.
Beezley
and others.

‡ 1 Str.
426, Sea-
good vs.
Neale.

plaintiff, are a ſufficient evidence, within the meaning of the ſtatute, of an agreement in writing ſigned by the defendants, to ſell the land to the higheſt bidder; § and as the plaintiff was the higheſt bidder, and tendered ſecurity for payment, purſuant to the written agreement of the defendants, he has a right of action againſt them, for refuſing a deed, which, by their agreement, they had promiſed to any perſon, complying with their terms.——If an action in ſuch caſe could not be ſuſtained, it would difcourage people from bidding at public auction, and render ineffectual the laws directing ſuch diſpoſition of eſtates.

Judge Ellsworth,—*diſſenting.*——1ſt. Becauſe the declaration is ill. It doth not appear that the plaintiff paid or offered to pay, or ſecure the ſum he bid for the land, nor that he bid any ſum that could have juſtified the adminiſtrators in paſſing a deed: Nor is there any averment of the value of the land, or any rule of damages given.——2d. The advertiſement is no evidence or memorandum of the agreement on which the action is grounded‡.—The agreement was made at the time the land was bid off, and was made and expreſſed on the one part by the bid made for the land, and on the other part by ſtriking it off.—Here the minds of the parties met, and the ſubſtance of the agreement, as thus expreſſed, was, that the plaintiff ſhould have the land for the ſum he had then bid for it, and that a deed ſhould be executed accordingly.——The advertiſement doth not expreſs this agreement, nor either part of it; nor was any reference had to the advertiſement in forming this agreement, farther, than as to the mode of payment.—That this ſale was at public auction, makes no difference.—It is as requiſite by the ſtatute that public ſales of land ſhould fhould be guarded as private ones; and it is as eafy to be done.—A memorandum of the fale might be taken in writing from the vendor, and Hobby, &c. would hardly be refufed, if required at the time of the fale or agreement.—I think the ftatute extends to this cafe, and that it has not been complied with.

MEAD *againſt* COGGSHALL.

THIS cafe was defaulted and heard in da- mages at the Court of Common Pleas.— After damages were affeffed, the plaintiff mo- ved for an appeal,—which was allowed.—At this Court the defendant pleaded in abatement of the appeal, on the ground that no appeal can be taken after a default.

Appeal lies after default and hearing in damages.

But it was held by the Court, that the appeal will lay, becaufe there was a *hearing* in the cafe, which brought it within the ftatute.

FITCH

1786.

FITCH *against* HALL.

A surrender of the principal in court by the bail, is to be proved only by the record, & cannot regularly be pleaded as matter in pais.

ACTION by the Sheriff on a bail bond.———— The defendant pleaded, that on the first day of April, A. D. 1779, while the action was pending in court, and before final judgement was rendered, the defendant did tender his principal to the plaintiff (he then being Sheriff, &c.) to be taken into custody in discharge of his bond; but the Sheriff refused to receive him. ————And that afterwards (to wit) on the first Tuesday of April, 1779, while the action was still pending against his principal, the defendant did deliver him up in open court in discharge of his bond, and requested to be discharged therefrom; but the Court neglected to make any record thereof, or to receive him into custody.

The plaintiff demurred specially.——1st. Because of duplicity——2d. For that the several matters pleaded were insufficient.

BY THE COURT.————The plea in bar is insufficient, not on the ground of duplicity; for though two matters are plead, they are not sufficient matters: Averments immaterial require no traverse, and are mere surplusage.——But the fault is in pleading a surrender of the principal in court as a matter *in pais*, and not a matter of record.‖———Every transaction in a court of record, pertaining to a process, of which the surrender of the principal in discharge of bail is one, regularly becomes a matter of record, and must be shewn by record only, and plead accordingly.

Judge DYER, *dissenting.*————It is agreed, that the producing the body of the principal, and delivering him up in court, is a legal fulfilment

‖ Croke Ja. 402.—— 3. Buls. 192, Austin vs. Monk —Hobart 210— 1. Levinz 211--Raymond 50-- Vin. A. P. B. A. 492, pl. 8.— Poph. 185, 186—Keb. 761, 816.

ment of the condition of the bail bond, and is all the bail can be obliged to do.—It is highly proper that the court caufe an entry to be made thereof, but it is what is not in the power of the bail to enjoin or enforce.—There is no pofitive law which requires it, or decidedly determines fuch entry to be the only evidence.—The admitting proof of the fact by verbal and other teftimony, does not contradict or oppofe any pofitive record, but goes only to prove a material fact where the record is wholly filent.— The bail exprefsly avers in his plea, that the principal was delivered up to the court in difcharge of his bond; and the law makes the ftrongeft conftruction in favour of the bail.—I am therefore of opinion the plea in bar is fufficient. When the bail has done all in his power, and what the law requires, ought he to be fubjected to pay over what was only the *juft debt* of the principal, meerly through the neglect of a clerk?

Note. This judgement was afterwards affirmed in the Supreme Court of Errors.

Fitch againft Hall.

BEERS *and Others againft* STRONG *and Wife.*

In Chancery.

THIS was a petition againft tenants in dower, to compel repairs to be made, agreeably to ftatute. The *heirs* and *widow* of *Abel Gunn,* deceafed, made partition of his eftate, by mutual agreement, under their hands and feals; by which, a certain tract of land and buildings, were

Statute provifions for compelling tenants in dower to repair, extends only, to dower affigned in the manner the ftatute prefcribes.

were apportioned to the *widow* as dower; and the buildings had not been kept in tenantable repair.

On demurrer,

THE WHOLE COURT HELD—That the *Statute proviſion* for compelling tenants in dower to re-pair, extends *only to dower aſſigned in the manner the Statute preſcribes.*—Here has been no ſuch aſſignment; nor is there any *dower.*—The wife of ſaid *Strong*, if ſhe has any thing in the lands in queſtion, has it by PURCHASE, and without other limitations or conditions than ſuch as are ſpecially provided in the *grant*, or *ſettlement* of the heirs under which ſhe holds.

Note. This judgement was afterwards affirm-ed in the Supreme Court of Errors.

STATE *of* CONNECTICUT *against* ELISHA ENOS.

INFORMATION at common law for uttering and putting off a counterfeit note, in
imitation of the notes iffued by the hon. *Robert
Morris,* Efq. fuperintendant of finance.—The
crime alledged to have been committed more
than one year before the filing of the infoim-
ation.

Mr. *Edwards,* counfel for the prifoner, pleaded the Statute of limitations; by which it is
enacted;—" That no perfon fhall be indicted,
" profecuted, informed againft, complained of,
" or compelled to anfwer before any Court, Af-
" fiftant or Juftice of the Peace within this ftate,
" for the breach of any penal law, or for other
" crime or mifdemeanor, by reafon whereof a
" *forfeiture* belongs to any public treafury, un-
" lefs the indictment, prefentment, information,
" or complaint be made and exhibited within
" one year after the offence is committed.

" And every fuch indictment, prefentment,
" information and complaint, that is not made
" and exhibited, as aforefaid, within the time
" limitted for the fame as aforefaid—fhall be
" void and of none effect.

" *Provided always,* That this act fhall not ex-
" tend to any capital offence; nor to any crime
" that may concern lofs of member, or banifh-
" ment, or any treachery againft this ftate, &c."

Mr. *Root,* attorney for the ftate, demurred.—
And on argument, the plea was adjudged fufficient;—for,

BY THE COURT.——The offence is within
the ftatute of limitations, being punifhable by
fine, or without, at the difcretion of the Court.
The conftruction of this ftatute has been liberal,
extending

The ftatute of limitations extends to offences which may be punifhed by fine, or otherwife at the difcreti- on of the court; as, fornication, riots, &c. and there- fore in an information at common law for paf- fing a coun- terfeit note, made in imitation of the notes iffu- ed by the fu- perintendant of finance.

extending it to offences which *might* be punished by fine, or without, at the difcretion of the
Court; as fornication, riots, &c. The exceptions in the act do not extend to this cafe; for,
by ftatute, no kind of forgery is punifhed with
fuch feverity as lofs of limb; and at common
law, punifhments are never more fevere than by
ftatute.

Judge Dyer, *diffenting*—1ft. Becaufe there
is no precedent, extending the ftatute of limitation, to cafes of this defcription, but the contrary.

2d. The ftatute referred to, which requires
the information to be within one year, is, " for
" the breach of any penal law, or for other
" crime or mifdemeanor, by reafon whereof a
" forfeiture belongs to any public treafury, &c.'
—On this information, there is no forfeiture to
any public treafury enjoined by any pofitive
law; therefore the cafe is not within the ftatute.

3d. Crimes, which may be punifhed by lofs
of member, banifhment, &c. as well as theft of
more than ten fhillings value, are exprefsly excepted by the ftatute. If the perfon fhould be
convicted on this information, the law admits of
a punifhment, which concerns lofs of member or
banifhment; therefore, this cafe was not within
the ftatute.

Bradley *and Others against* Blodget.

Lands fold,
and convey-
ed by deed,
defcribing
the metes,
bounds,

ACTION on the cafe, ftating that the plaintiffs purchafed of the defendant a certain
tract of land fuppofed to contain fixty acres, de-
lines and fuppofed quantity; a verbal promife at the fame time, to pay the grantee
for all that it fhall fall fhort on menfuration; adjudged to be within the ftatute
ef frauds and perjury.

scribed by certain metes, bounds and lines.—
That, at the time of sale and delivery of the
deed, the defendant promised, if on actual men-
suration said tract of land should fall short of
sixty acres, he would satisfy the plaintiffs for the
deficiency; and afterwards, by an accurate sur-
vey and menfuration, there proved to be but
forty acres.

1786.

Bradly, &c
against
Blodget.

The defendant demurred specially, and for
cause assigned—

1. That the plaintiffs might have their remedy on the covenants contained in the deed.

2. That it appears from the declaration, the
plaintiffs took a deed of said land, describing the
quantity and bounds, and no parole contract or
agreement, beyond that contained in the deed,
is admissible in law.

3. The declaration shows, that the plaintiffs
saw said land and received a deed, giving a rule
to find the quantity; of consequence, there was
no deception.

4. That the promise declared upon, is a parole
promise, concerning the sale of lands, and therefore within the statute of frauds and perjuries.

The plaintiffs joined in demurrer, and the
declaration was adjudged insufficient.

By Law, *Chief Justice,* Dyer *and* Pitkin,
Judges.——This declaration is insufficient on
two grounds :—

1. Because the plaintiffs might have known
the quantity of land before they paid the money, it being particularly described by metes
and bounds; and no pretence but that the title
well passed, or that the lines therein described
fell short, or that the angles are misdescribed.—
And as the deed contained in it demonstrative
evidence of its contents, any parole contract,
contradicting the same, or relative thereto, is
inadmissible.

2. Because

2. Becauſe it does not appear that the agreement was reduced to writing, and therefore void by the ſtatute of frauds and perjuries; as the defendant in his ſpecial demurrer, points out the contract, as coming within the ſtatute, on the ground of being a parole contract, and the plaintiffs not replying over and alledging it to be otherwiſe, it muſt be preſumed, the promiſe was not committed to writing.

Judge SHERMAN, *diſſenting.*——The agreement is not within the ſtatute of frauds and perjuries, it being a promiſe only to pay back a ſum of money, overpaid for the land, if, upon actual menſuration, it fell ſhort of its ſuppoſed contents.——And the agreement appears to be legal and reaſonable, for the price of the land was, by agreement of the parties, to be in proportion to the contents which could not be known, but by its being ſurveyed by ſome ſkilful ſurveyor, which the parties might well poſtpone to ſome convenient time; and if, when aſcertained, it appeared that more than the price agreed on had been paid, the ſurplus ought to be refunded.——And if the promiſe had been within the ſtatute of frauds and perjuries, and in writing, it need not have been ſet forth in the declaration, but might have been given in evidence on the general iſſue; and no advantage can be taken of the omiſſion on a general or ſpecial demurrer. ——*Raym.* 450; 451—2 *Jones,* 158. S. C.— 1 *Bac. Abr.* 75—*Buller's Niſi Prius,* 275.

BRINLEY *against* AVERY.

THIS was an action on the case, brought by
George Brinley, Esq. Commissary General
of the British province of Nova Scotia, founded
on a written agreement.

The defendant pleaded in abatement, that the
plaintiff is an alien, born in the dominions of the
king of Great-Britain, an inhabitant of Halifax,
in said dominions, a subject within the allegiance of said king, and without the allegiance of
the state of Connecticut, and of the United
States of America; and banished and proscribed
by the commonwealth of Massachusetts, and at
the time of the date of said contract and supposed breach thereof, both the plaintiff and defendant were inhabitants of said Halifax, subjects
of said king of Great-Britain; both under the
allegiance of said king, and owing no allegiance
to this state, or to said United States. And the
defendant at said date, and for more than twenty
five years before the same was, and had been, an
inhabitant of said Nova-Scotia, and subject of
said king. And that said Halifax, at the time
of the date of said contract was, and ever had
been, governed by the laws and statutes of the
kingdom of Great-Britain, and not by the laws
and statutes of the state of Connecticut; and said
contract, and all transactions between the plaintiff and defendant, ought to be tried and determined in and by the courts of said king of Great-
Britain, according to the laws, statutes and usages of said kingdom, and not in and by any
court in the state of Connecticut, or according
to the laws and usages of said state. And said
contract was made at said Halifax, and to have
been there performed, during said time when

An action is not maintainable in this state upon a contract made in a foreign country, between citizens of that country, and to be there performed.

D   the

the plaintiff and defendant were inhabitants of
ſaid Halifax.

2. That by the law of nations, no ſuch action
can be ſupported, nor can the ſubjects of this
ſtate, by the laws of England, or of other nations, maintain any action againſt each other on
any contract made, or for any injury done, within the juriſdiction of ſaid ſtate, in any court in
the Britiſh dominions, or in any other foreign
court.

3. That the final judgement given by this
court, in the preſent action, would be no bar to
the plaintiff in commencing and proſecuting a
ſecond action for the ſame cauſe, matter and
thing, in any of the courts in ſaid province of
Nova-Scotia, or ſaid kingdom of Great-Britain,
nor prevent the plaintiff from recovering a ſecond judgement thereon againſt the defendant,
his goods and eſtate yet remaining in ſaid Halifax.

Replication.————That ſaid king and kingdom of Great-Britain, to whom the plaintiff was,
and is a ſubject, and owed his allegiance, are,
and were at the time of ſaid contract, at amity,
and in league with this ſtate, and the United
States of America; and their ſubjects have
right, by the treaty of peace between ſaid king
of Great-Britain and the United States, and by
the laws of nations, and of this ſtate, to maintain actions in the courts of common law in this
ſtate, for the recovery of their dues, againſt the
citizens of this ſtate, or others that are ſubjects
of the king and kingdom of Great-Britain, who
may come to reſide here, and take up their
abode in this ſtate with their property and effects,
in any action that is perſonal and tranſitory.——
And that the defendant was an inhabitant born,
and reſided a long time in this ſtate, and after
many years abſence therefrom, at ſaid Halifax,

he

Brinley
againſt
Avery.

he returned into ſaid ſtate in the year 1785, with his property and effects, and ever ſince has here reſided, and taken up his abode in this ſtate, and both his perſon and eſtate are amenable to the laws and courts of the ſame.

To this there was a demurrer and joinder in demurrer;—and the plea in abatement ruled ſufficient.

WOOSTER *and* WOOSTER *againſt* PARSONS.

Wlicn an action is bro't before any court of inferior and limited jurdiction, the declaration ought to aver expreſſly, that the cauſe of action aroſe within the juriſdiction of the court.

ERROR from the city court in Middletown.——The defendant in error brought his action on a promiſſory note, dated at New-Haven the 7th day of June, 1784, before the city court in Middletown, and obtained judgement by default.——Errors aſſigned,

1. That it appears by the records, that ſaid note was executed before the city of Middletown was incorporated, and before the granting the charter incorporating the ſame;—ſaid charter of incorporation being granted by the General Aſſembly, holden at Hartford on the ſecond Thurſday of May, 1784; which Aſſembly was ſitting at the time when ſaid note was executed.

2. That ſaid note was not executed within the limits of ſaid city of Middletown, but in the town of New-Haven: And the cauſe of action did not ariſe within the limits of the city of Middletown.

3. That it doth not appear by ſaid record, that ſaid note was executed in ſaid city of Middletown, but that the ſame was executed without the limits of ſaid city.

The

The defendant in error demurred ſpecially, and for cauſe aſſigned, that ſaid writ contains an aſſignment of errors both in law and in fact, which cannot be joined in one writ of error: For, it is aſſigned for error, that ſaid note was executed before the incorporation of ſaid city of Middletown; and alſo that ſaid note was not executed within the limits of ſaid city, but in the town of New-Haven: Both which are aſſignments of errors in fact, not appearing on the record, and triable only by iſſues in fact.——And the plaintiffs further aſſign, that it does not appear by the record, that ſaid note was executed in ſaid city of Middletown, but that the ſame was executed out of the limits of ſaid city.—Which is an aſſignment of error in law, and triable only by iſſue in law.

Second, The defendant in error, by proteſtation that ſaid facts, by the plaintiffs in error aſſigned, are not true, ſaith, that ſaid errors in fact contain only the ſubſtance of a plea to the juriſdiction of ſaid city court, which the plaintiffs in error ought by law to have pleaded and excepted againſt before ſaid city court, and having then waved the ſame, they cannot by law aſſign ſaid matters in error;—and that ſaid errors aſſigned are in contradiction of the record.

Third, That ſaid aſſignment of error in law, alledging that it does not appear by ſaid record that ſaid note was executed in ſaid city of Middletown, but that the ſame was executed out of the limits of ſaid city, is an allegation contrary to ſaid record, and cannot by law be aſſigned in error.

Fourth, That no matter or thing, in ſaid writ of error aſſigned, is ſufficient to warrant the reverſal of ſaid judgement.

On argument of *this caſe*, by Mr. *Parſons* and Mr. *Trumbull*, for the defendant in error, and

by

by Mr. *Ingerfoll* and Mr. *Chauncey* for the plaintiffs, judgement was reverfed.

By **Dyer**, Sherman and Pitk4n, *Judges.*

1. When an action is brought before any
court of limited and inferior jurifdiction, the
declaration ought to aver exprefsly, that the
caufe of action arofe within the jurifdiction of
the court;§ and the place fhould be particularly alledged: Neither of which was done with
fufficient certainty in the prefent cafe. The
note on which, &c. is alledged to have been
executed in the city *aforefaid* ;—the *city of New-
Haven,* and the city of *Middletown,* having been
both before mentioned—therefore uncertain to
which the reference was intended.—(*See Coke on
Littleton,* 20, *a.*)—" If a leafe for life is made
" to *A.* remainder in tail to *B.* remainder to *C.*
" *informa prædicta,* the remainder to *C.* is void
" for uncertainty."†——This author makes a
diftinction between *prædicta,* and fome other relative terms, which he fuppofes commonly refer
to the laft antecedent; but that the rule admits
of many exceptions.*—If fuch an uncertain reference would render a grant void, which would
be fupported, if by any reafonable conftruction
it could be made certain, it muft *á fortiori* be
fatal to a declaration, which is to be conftrued
moft ftrongly againft the declarant. If the note
had been executed in the city of Middletown,
the allegation ought to have been " *in the city
of Middletown aforefaid, within the jurifdiction
of the faid court.*"

§ 2 Lord
Raymond,
1310.

† 2 Ld.
Raymond,
886 to 890,
Judgment
arrefted for
a like un-
certainty.

‡ 3 Salk.
199.
Hard. 77.
Dyer, 17.

2. The

* The reafon of the diftinction is, that *aforefaid,* may
with propriety relate to any term, that has been before ufed
in the fame inftrument or writing, however remote; but
the other relative terms there mentioned, can only relate
to fome word in the fame fentence.

2. The note on which, &c. is dated the 7th of June, 1784, and the ſeſſion of the legiſlature at which the law was enacted, for incorporating the city of Middletown, ended the 11th of the ſame June, as appears of record: And, therefore, the cauſe of action aroſe before the juriſdiction of the city of Middletown commenced; for laws in this ſtate are not in force till the end of the ſeſſion in which they are paſſed, unleſs by ſpecial proviſion in the ſtatute; for during the whole of the ſeſſion, they are ſubject to alteration, or to be totally negatived and not entered on record; whereas after the end of the ſeſſion, they become matters of record, and cannot be altered or repealed, but by a new act paſſed and recorded: Nor would it be reaſonable that people ſhould be affected by laws before they are publiſhed, which is not done (except in ſpecial inſtances) before the riſing of the legiſlature.

3. As to the exception in the defendants plea, that *errors* in *law* and *errors* in *fact* are joined in the writ; the plaintiffs have aſſigned no facts in error, upon which they rely, but ſuch as appear of record: And an aſſignment of errors in *fact*, not properly aſſignable, together with ſufficient errors in law, will not vitiate the writ.

Therefore, the judgement of the city court was reverſed.

LAW, *Chief Juſtice, and* ELLSWORTH, *diſſenting.*——As to the firſt exception in error, " that " the plaintiff, in the original ſuit, has not al- " ledged, with ſufficient certainty, that the cauſe " of action aroſe within the city of Middletown."

The averment is, that " the note was execu- " ted within the city *aforeſaid*." And the city of Middletown was the next antecedent. And the rule in pleadings, as in grammar, is, that relation muſt always be to the next antecedent, unleſs the ſenſe hinders; which in this inſtance
cannot

1786.

Wooft. &c.
againft
Parfons.

cannot be pretended.—*Hardrefs*, 77—3. *Sal-keld*, 199. It has formerly been held by fome. that *prædictum* was of lefs certain relation than. *idem*; but there appears no reafon for the dif-tinction,-and it hath not been kept up. And in *Rhodes* and *Coles* cafe, 2. Lord *Raymond*, 886, which turned upon the reference of *prædictum* or *aforefaid*, Chief *Juftice Holt* held.it.muft be. to the next antecedent; and the cafe was finally adjudged according to, his opinion. Certainty, to common intendment, is fufficient in fupport of a judgement; for *femper prefumiter, pro fententia.*—And, though *formerly* the courts of Weftminfter-hall would prefume nothing in favour of inferior jurifdictions, or the regularity of their proceedings, of late years they. have prefumed liberally in fupport of them.—1. Ld. *Raymond*, 80—and *Cowper* 18.

With regard to the fecond exception, " that " the caufe of action arofe before the city of " Middletown was incorporated."—

The act of incorporation, as appears from the journals of the Houfe of Affembly, paffed and was compleated the 24th day of May, fourteen days preceding the date of the note : And it was afterwards revocable only as every ftatute is, by a concurrence of both branches of the Legiflature. And altho' had it been a penal or man-datory act, it would-not have fo had effect as to become obligatory on the citizens of the ftate at large, until they had had means of the know-ledge of it, which ordinarily would not have been till the rifing of the Affembly, and the re-turn of their reprefentatives; yet being in na-ture of a grant, and there being no time men-tioned therein when it fhould begin to take ef-fect, it took effect immediately; and the jurif-diction it gave of fuits, where the caufe of ac-tion " *fhould arife*," &c. has relation to the time
of

of the act's paſſing;—unleſs, according to the Britiſh rule of conſtruing ſtatutes in ſuch caſes, it ſhall, in amplification of the grant or authority, have relation to the firſt day of the ſeſſion in which it paſſed.—1 *Roll. Abr.* 465—4 *Inſt.* 25, 27—*Hob.* 309. As to the objection to this conſtruction of the act, that it may ſubject cauſes to the deciſion of a forum which the parties, at the time the cauſe of action aroſe, did not contemplate—it is of very little weight;—as it does not affect the rule or principles of the deciſion :—And it has been always diſregarded by the legiſlature in the inſtitution of new courts ; even where they have gone ſo far as to change the mode of trial from a jury to a ſingle miniſter, as in the late enlargement of the juriſdiction of juſtices of the peace.

It appears, therefore, to us from the record, that the cauſe of action aroſe within the juriſdiction of the city-court ; both in point of time and locality ;—and that, that court did not err in taking cognizance of the cauſe.

HUNTINGTON

Huntington *against* Jones.

ERROR from the court of common pleas. ——The cafe was, *Jones* recovered judgement againft *Huntington*, in an action of troyer, had execution, and committed him to goal.—— *Huntington* was a poor prifoner, and unable to difcharge the debt.—*Jones* preferred his petition to the court of common pleas, that *Huntington* might be affigned in fervice a fufficient length of time to fatisfy faid execution, and additional coft.—The petition was founded on that part of the ftatute *concerning arrefts and imprifonment,* which enacts, " That, if no other " means can be found to pay the debt for which " fuch debtor is imprifoned, the debtor fhall fa- " tisfy the fame by fervice, if the creditor defire " it, and the court fhall judge it reafonable; in " which cafe the fuperior or county court fhall " have power to order and difpofe of fuch debtor " in fervice, for the purpofe aforefaid, to fome " inhabitant of this ftate, whether the execu- " tion by which he is held iffued from fuch " court, or not.

" *Provided always,* that no court in this ftate " fhall, in any civil cafe, affign or difpofe of " any perfon in fervice, until fuch court is fa- " tisfied, by the oath of the parties or other- " ways, that faid debtor hath not eftate fuffici- " cient to pay the debt for which he is holden " by execution, except fuch neceffaries as are " by law exempted from being taken by execu- " tion; and the debt for which he is holden is " really and *bona fide* due, on good confider- " ation."

Huntington, and his other judgement creditors, upon whofe debts he was likewife impri-

E   foned,

foned, moved that *Jones's* petition might not
be granted: They urged, that each creditor
had an equal right to the ſervice of the debtor;
that his life being uncertain, if preference ſhould
be given to *one,* the *other* creditors might loſe
their debts.—*Huntington* ſuggeſted to the court,
that the judgement of *Jones* againſt him was un-
juſtly obtained, and moved that both might be
examined under oath, as to the juſtice of the
debt; which the court refuſed, and difpoſed of
Huntington, in ſervice to *Jones,* the creditor,
his heirs and aſſigns, for the term of two years
and ſix months, in diſcharge of the debt.

Six exceptions in error were taken to this
deciſion of the court of common pleas:—

1. That the court ought not to have aſſigned
him in ſervice for the debt of *Jones* only, when
he was confined in priſon by force of other judg-
ments in favour of other creditors.

2. That agreeably to the juſt conſtruction of
the ſtatute, regulating the proceedings in ſuch
caſes, *Huntington* had right to teſtify under oath,
and to an examination of the adverſe party reſpecting the juſtice of ſaid original demand;
which was denied in this caſe.

3. That it was not agreeable to the true ſpirit
and meaning of the ſtatute, that *Huntington,* under the circumſtances, ſhould have been aſſigned in ſervice.

4. That the court erred in extending the ſervice to ſuch a length of time.

5. That the firſt judgement was rendered in
an action of trover, for the ſatisfaction of which,
the law will not juſtify an aſſignment in ſervice.

6. That the court erred in aſſigning ſaid *Huntington* to the heirs and aſſigns of ſaid *Jones.*

On the laſt error alledged, the judgement
was reverſed: For,

By

Huntingt.
againſt
Jones.

BY THE WHOLE COURT.——The binding here is not only to the perſon named, but alſo to his *heirs and aſſigns*: Whereas, by the ſtatute, the right of ſervice is perſonal, and extends only to the maſter named and approved by the court, who are to regard as well the condition and character of the perſon to whom the aſſignment is made, as of the perſon aſſigned.—— The proviſion of law for aſſigning debtors in ſervice being an abridgment of perſonal liberty, requires caution in exerciſe, and is not to be enlarged by implication.

THOMSON *againſt* WALES *and* MOOR.

No appeal lies from the deciſion of a lower court on a book debt action, if the ſum alledged as debt, does not exceed twenty pounds, although the ſum demanded in damages, exceed that ſum.

ERROR from the court of common pleas. ——*Thomſon* brought his action of book-debt againſt *Wales* and *Moor*, adminiſtrators on the eſtate of *James M'Neil*, declaring for a debt of 20*l*. and demanding in damage 24*l*.—The general iſſue was plead, and judgement for the defendant.—The plaintiff moved for an appeal, which was denied.

The error aſſigned was, that the ſum demanded being more than 20*l*. the plaintiff was entitled to an appeal; for the court could not determine that the jury would not find more than 20*l*. or even the whole ſum demanded, in damage.

Judgement affirmed.

·BY THE COURT.——No appeal lies. The words of the ſtatute granting appeals, are, " in " which the value of the debt, damage, or mat- " ter in diſpute, doth exceed the value of 20*l*. " &c."—In this caſe the debt demanded, which is laid at 20*l*. only, is the matter in diſpute;

And

1786.

Thomson
against
Wales.

and the conclusion in damages but a matter of form. And if interest is to be challenged in an action of book-debt, it is regularly to be charged, and made parcel of the debt alledged, that the adverse party may have notice of it upon oyer; and we have no practice of entering a judgement for a sum in debt, and a further sum for interest or damages, for the detention of the debt. The 20l. the sum alledged as debt in this case, is all that judgement could have been given for, and was the whole matter in dispute.

Judge DYER—*dissenting.*——The statute limits to a final decision of the court of common pleas, such actions wherein the matter in demand does not exceed the value of 20l.—The magnitude of the demand, is to be ascertained by the *jury*, and not by the *court*, unless by agreement of parties; and since the plaintiff, in this action, has demanded a sum for interest or damage, exceeding the stated debt, the question, whether he shall recover more than the debt so stated, he has a right to have determined by jury; and until that is determined, the court cannot legally deprive the party of an appeal.

BACKUS *against* CLEAVELAND.

An existing claim against the estate of a deceased person, under such circumstances that the amount cannot not be ascertained within the time limited by the court of probate for exhibiting the claims of creditors to such estate; such claim is not foreclosed, but may be exhibited and recovered afterwards, if the administrator have estate in his hands.

THIS was a *scire facias*, for the affirmance of a judgement against the defendant, as *administrator* on the estate of *Aron Cleaveland.*

The defendant pleaded, that the court of probate issued an order, that within a limited time all claims against said estate should be ex-

1786.

hibited to the defendant, or be forever barred; and that due notice thereof had been given to the plaintiff, but he did not exhibit his claim within the term limited.

The plaintiff replied, that he brought his writ of error against the *inteftate* to the *fuperior court*, in March 1785, and obtained a reverfal of an erroneous judgement of the court of common pleas.—That the *inteftate* then being in full life, entered his action in the docket of faid *fuperior court*, which was continued till September 1785. —In April 1785, the faid *Aron* died; and at faid September term, the defendant appeared and moved for leave to profecute faid action on the part of faid deceafed, which was allowed.— Said caufe was adjourned till December 1785, when final judgement was rendered in favour of faid *Aron, deceafed*, for forty-nine pounds and fix-pence lefs than the fum of the former judgement rendered by the *court of common pleas*, which had been reverfed.—Which fum was reftored to the plaintiff as his damage by reafon of faid erroneous judgement, and which is the demand in queftion.—That this demand could not have been exhibited within the time limited, becaufe it was then pending in court; all which the defendant well knew.—And that the defendant now holds in his hands eftate of faid deceafed, much more than fufficient to difcharge the prefent debt.

To this there was a demurrer, and joinder in demurrer—and the replication was adjudged fufficient: For,

By the whole Court.——The amount of the plaintiff's claim against the eftate of the deceafed, could not be afcertained until the final judgement in the caufe then pending before the fuperior court, as mentioned in the plaintiff's reply; which judgement was not rendered until

3 Wilfon, 13.
Chilton vs Whiffie.
2. Strange, 867.
Tully vs Sparkes.
2. Lord Raymond, 1546,1570.

Backus
againſt
Cleavland

2. Strange,
1043.
Hockley
vs Merry.
3. Wilſon,
262.
Goddard
vs Van-
derheyden.

til after the expiration of the term limited by the *court of probate,* for exhibiting the claims of the creditors to ſaid eſtate.

It appears by the pleadings, that the defendant well knew the demand that the plaintiff had againſt the eſtate, and the circumſtances attending the ſame, and that he has ſufficient eſtate of the deceaſed in his hands to diſcharge it: Therefore the plaintiff is not by law forecloſed from recovering his debt according to the true intent of the ſtatute in that caſe provided.

N. B. This judgement was afterwards affirmed in the ſupreme court of errors.

ADAMS *againſt* CLEAVELAND.

IN this caſe the ſame point was determined as in the caſe of *Backus* againſt *Cleaveland,* on ſimilar pleadings.

FITCH *againſt* HUNTINGTON.——*In Error.*

After the average is ſtruck on an inſolvent eſtate, no future intereſt can ariſe on ſuch average, as relative to the eſtate; but if the adminiſtrator ſo conduct as to ſubject himſelf perſonally to the payment of intereſt, the action muſt be brought accordingly.

HUNTINGTON brought his action to the court of common pleas, on a promiſſory note, againſt *Fitch,* adminiſtrator on the eſtate of *Azel Fitch,* deceaſed.——*Fitch* pleaded in abatement, that the eſtate of ſaid deceaſed was duly repreſented inſolvent (and in fact proved unable to pay more than one ſhilling and ſixpence on the pound.)——That commiſſioners were duly appointed to receive and examine the claims upon ſaid eſtate, who gave notice of their appointment and powers, according to law; and that the plaintiff neglected to exhibit his demand, until the expiration of ſaid commiſſion, miffion, and a final fettlement and quietus was granted upon faid adminiftration.

The plaintiff replied, that in January 1770, he exhibited his faid claim to the commiffioners on faid eftate, in the life of their commiffion, who allowed the fame, and made return thereof to the court of probate; which return was accepted by the faid court.

Upon the facts ftated in the replication, iffue was joined; and a verdict for the plaintiff. Mr. *Larrabee* and Mr. *Biſſel* moved in arreft, and for caufe alledged—

1. That the jury, in their affeffment of damages, had allowed to the plaintiff the intereft on the average fum of his debt, from the time it was prefented to the commiffioners; which was illegal.

2. That the original note on which, &c. having been exhibited to the commiffioners, and by them allowed and afcertained againft the eftate of faid deceafed, no action is now fuftainable on faid original note.—And that there can be no foundation in law, for a recovery of damages by the plaintiff, but upon a neglect of payment by the defendant, as adminiftrator.

Mr. *Swift* and Mr. *Spalding* replied, that the demand againft the eftate of faid *Azel* deceafed, was a note of hand on intereft, and that faid average ought to have been paid in the month of January 1770, but the defendant, regardlefs of his duty as adminiftrator, took all the eftate into his poffeffion, and had ever fince had the ufe and benefit thereof, and had always refufed to difcharge faid debt; and that the jury allowed no more than the lawful intereft of the plaintiff's average from the time it ought to have been paid.

The court of common pleas eftablifhed this verdict, and rendered judgement thereon.

Judgement was reverfed.   BY

Fitch
again/l
Huntingt.

BY THE WHOLE COURT.——Interest, upon the plaintiff's average, was allowed out of the estate of the deceased.   This would work injustice to the other creditors, who would thereby be cut short of their average.—If an administrator upon an insolvent estate, after the average is struck, makes himself liable for interest, it is his *own estate* he subjects, and not *that* of the deceased ; and the action and judgement should accord with the circumstance of the administrator's *personal* liableness.

———————————

•

BUEL *against* METCALF.——*In Error.*

Goods are taken by attachment and delivered to B. he promises to re-deliver them on demand ; if they be not demanded within sixty days after final judgment in the action on which they are attached, B. may restore them to the original owner, and shall not be liable on his promise to the officer.

METCALF brought his action against *Buel*, to the court of common pleas, on a receipt executed by the defendant to the plaintiff, as constable, for goods taken by attachment, containing a promise to re-deliver said goods on demand, for the purpose of responding the judgment on the writ of attachment.

The defendant pleaded, that he held said goods, and was ready to re-deliver them to the plaintiff at all times, until the expiration of more than sixty days after final judgement on said writ of attachment ; that no demand was made for said goods, and in consequence of the premises, he restored them to the original owner.

On demurrer to this plea, judgement was rendered for the plaintiff.

The plaintiff in error took two exceptions to this judgement—

1. That the declaration was insufficient, as it appeared from the face of it, that execution was

not

not issued till more than sixty days after final judgement was rendered, and therefore the estate taken was discharged, and the defendant not holden to deliver it.

2. That the plea contained ample matter to discharge the defendant from his liability to said suit.

The judgement was reversed.

BY THE WHOLE COURT.——The execution was not taken out till more than sixty days after the judgement, beyond the expiration of which time the attachment could not hold the property, and it became thereupon the duty of the officer, or of whoever held the property under him, to restore it to the debtor (as the receipt-man has done) and he would have been liable in trover had he refused.

KIMBALL against CADY.

ERROR, from a decree of the court of common pleas, on a petition for a new trial.——Kimball brought his action against Cady on a promissary note to the court of common pleas in August 1781.—The defendant pleaded a tender made in April 1779.—The plaintiff replied, that the money tendered, and now offered, consisted of continental bills of credit, which were not at the time of tender, and have never since been, at the value of one thirtieth part of the debt contracted and promised in said note.

. To this there was a demurrer, and judgement for the defendant.

Kimball, the plaintiff, petitioned for a new trial. He relied on the statute passed in Octo-

A petition for new trial is matter of discretion with the court to which it is prefered, to grant or negative; therefore Error cannot be predicated on such decision.

F   ber

ber 1782, which enacts, " That in all actions
" brought before any of the ſuperior or county
" courts in this ſtate, (either by original writ,
" appeal, or writ of error) for the recovery of
" any debt due by bond, note, or book account,
" contracted before or on the ſeventh day of
" of *January*, 1780, and where the defendant in
" ſuch action has, between the firſt day of *Sep-*
" *tember*, 1777, and the 18th day of *March*,
" 1780, made a tender of a ſum in *continental*
" *bills of credit*, to the creditor or creditors, in
" ſatisfaction of the debt demanded, and the
" creditor refuſed the ſame; then, and in every
" ſuch caſe, the court before whom each action
" may be brought, are hereby authorized to di-
" rect ſuch caſe to be heard and determined by
" reference thereof to indifferent perſons, to be
" mutually choſen by the contending parties;
" and in caſe they or their attornies ſhall neglect
" or refuſe to agree on ſuch references, the ſaid
" court are authorized to determine ſuch cauſe
" according to the rules of equity, taking all cir-
" cumſtances into conſideration:' Which ſaid
" referees ſo choſen as aforeſaid, ſhall hear and
" determine ſuch cauſe, as to them ſhall appear
" juſt and equitable, taking into conſideration
" all the circumſtances thereof, and make re-
" turn to the ſame court where ſaid cauſe ſhall
" be depending; who, unleſs ſufficient objec-
" tions be offered againſt ſuch return, ſhall ac-
" cept the ſame, and render judgement thereon
" accordingly,'——And on this ground he alledged, that a repleader ought to be granted;
for that he had miſtook his plea, in that he
did not traverſe the defendant's plea in bar, and
thereby open the ſubject of enquiry at large, to
the court.——That the ſtatute enables the court,
in ſuch caſe, to give the cauſe an equitable conſideration, and adjudge to the plaintiff what was
equitable

equitable and juſt, notwithſtanding the tender.

Three exceptions were taken to this petition, at the court of common pleas, by way of abatement:—

1. That the petitioner had not laid a profert of the legal proceedings mentioned in his petition.

2. That nothing appeared by the petition, but that compleat juſtice had taken place.

3. That the ſtatute mentioned in the petition did not exiſt until long after the final trial; therefore not applicable to this caſe.

The exceptions were adjudged ſufficient, and the petition diſmiſſed: And the decree of the court of common pleas being examined on this writ of error, was affirmed.

BY THE WHOLE COURT.——There are two grounds for affirming the deciſion of the court of common pleas:—

1. If the petition was for a new trial, it was matter of diſcretion with the court to which it was prefered, to grant or negative, and error cannot be predicated upon ſuch deciſion.

2. The petition cannot be ſuſtained on the ſtatute for the equitable deciſion of tenders in certain caſes, as there had been a judgement at law: For the proviſion of the ſtatute extends not to caſes adjudged and cloſed at law, but to caſes open and proſecuting at law, and is expreſsly limited to actions pending by original writ, appeal, or writ of error.—An extenſion of the ſtatute retroſpectively to overthrow judgements that have been rendered and acquieſced in at law, would be very inconvenient, and the words of the act will not admit of ſuch a conſtruction.

ROGERS

Rogers *againſt* Hemsted *and Others.*

THIS was an action on a written agreement between the plaintiff and defendants, ſtating, " That whereas they were jointly con-" cerned in the capture of a ſmall boat and ſe-" veral cattle, in April, 1783, which were li-" beled and condemned to the uſe of the cap-" tors, and diſtribution made accordingly :—" They therefore, jointly and ſeverally engaged " to pay the plaintiff (in whoſe name ſaid con-" demnation was had) their reſpective propor-" tions of any future expence that might ariſe in " the premiſes."——Subſequent to this agree-ment, one *Randal* claimed the property of the boat and cattle mentioned in the writing; for which he inſtituted a ſuit againſt the plaintiff, and recovered about ſixty pounds.—This action was brought to recover of the defendants their reſpective proportions of ſaid expenditure.

The defendants pleaded a diſcharge from the plaintiff, which was recited in theſe words——" Received of *Daniel Harris* twenty eight ſilver " dollars, on account of a boat and cattle taken " from *Randal* the 4th of April, 1783, and con-" demned to ſaid *Rogers*, and ſince ſaid *Randal* " has got an execution againſt ſaid *Rogers* for " ſixty ſeven pounds;—and this is *Daniel Har-*" *ris's* receipt for his part of ſaid execution."

To this plea the plaintiff demurred general-ly.——And,

By the whole Court.——This plea is inſufficient.——This receipt was not in full of the execution, but only of ſuch part or propor-tion of it as *Harris* had received of the proper-ty condemned. He, with the reſt of the de-fendants, as they were jointly and ſeverally bound for each others like proportions, remain-ed holden for the reſidue of the execution.

Huntington *and Others against* Carpenter.

THIS was an action of disseisin, brought by
the inhabitants of the town of Norwich,
against the defendant, as lessee of the first ecclesiastical society in said town.—On special pleadings, the case was thus stated for the decision of
court :———

The town of Norwich, before the year 1695,
constituted but one parish or ecclesiastical society; and the inhabitants transacted their town
and parochial business at the same meetings. In
June, 1765, they appointed a committee to purchase lands for the use and accommodation of
a gospel minister amongst them: The committee purchased of *Stephen Gifford* the lands in
question, and took a deed of bargain and sale,
expressed to be, " to the inhabitants of the *town*
" of Norwich, their heirs, successors and af-
" signs." In December, 1697, the inhabitants
of the town, by a vote, levied a tax on them-
selves, for the purposes of discharging the minister's salary, paying for the land purchased of
Gifford, and defraying other parish charges.
The lands in question were immediately applied to the use for which they were purchased,
and have ever since been applied to the use of
the ministry in the first society in Norwich.—
The inhabitants of the town, by vote, in December, 1701, sequestered for the use of the ministry, other lands adjoining the lands in question, and gave the whole the name of the Par-
sonage Lot.—In 1716, by act of assembly, two
other ecclesiastical societies were incorporated
from the town of Norwich, called the *East-
Farms* and the *West-Farms*; after which (to wit)
in July, 1717, Mr. *Benjamin Lord* was settled
in the ministry in the old or first society in said
town ;

town; and in Auguft, 1717, the faid fociety, by vote, granted to him the lands in queftion, for the term of his miniftry; which he held until the time of his death, which happened in April, 1784.

The proprietors of the townfhip of Norwich, in fundry legal meetings, did grant, lay out, and fequefter, fundry tracts of land in the focieties of the Eaft and Weft Farms, for the fupport of the miniftry in thofe two parifhes.

That the defendant holds the demanded premifes by force of a leafe from the firft ecclefiaftical fociety in Norwich, for term of years, not yet expired, and bearing date before the plaintiffs' writ.

There was a demurrer to the replication, and joinder in demurrer—and judgement for the defendant.

By the Court.——The inhabitants of each town in this ftate (not divided into focieties) are by law a corporation for the purpofe of fupporting public worfhip, and the gofpel miniftry, as well as for civil purpofes; and in their corporate capacity, have power to receive and hold eftates real and perfonal, for faid ufes, and to call and fettle minifters, build meeting houfes, &c.

2. The name and defcription by which they receive eftates, and tranfact bufinefs in their ecclefiaftical and civil capacity, is the fame (to wit) *the inhabitants of the town of*, &c.

3. When part of the inhabitants of fuch town are conftituted a new and diftinct fociety, the remaining inhabitants are by law confidered, for ecclefiaftical purpofes, as the fame corporation, having continuance and fucceffion, by the name of *the firft fociety*, which before exifted by the name of, *the inhabitants of the town*, and as holding the meeting houfe, and all other eftates that the inhabitants of fuch town received, acquired

quired and held, for any of the ufes for which
focieties are conftituted, and as bound to perform all the contracts and agreements made by
the inhabitants of fuch town, with the minifter,
for his fupport, or refpecting any other matter
proper to a fociety.—This opinion is fupported
by former adjudications, and univerfal cuftom.

4. In the prefent cafe, it appears from the records of the votes and proceedings of the town
of Norwich, recited in the pleadings, that the
land in queftion was purchafed when there was
but one ecclefiaftical fociety in the town, with
exprefs intention to be applied in fupporting the
gofpel miniftry.—That the purchafe money was
collected in the fame tax with the minifter's fa-
lary: And although the deed from *Gifford* does
not mention the ufe for which faid land was purchafed, and contains fimply a fale and transfer,
for a valuable confideration, as it was out of his
power, as grantor, to direct the ufe; yet it appears, that the grantees acting in the fame capacity as when calling and fettling a minifter, applied the ufe of faid land toward the fupport of
feveral fucceffive minifters of the gofpel, in that
part of the town of Norwich which is now called the firft fociety, for a term of more than
eighty years: That it was early called the par-
fonage land, and has never been applied to any
other ufe;—And therefore ought to be confidered as purchafed and held by the fame corporation that is now called the firft fociety in the
town of Norwich.

5. As it clearly appears, that it was the intention of the inhabitants of the town of Norwich (in whatever capacity they acted) to ap-
propriate faid land for the ufe and fupport of
the miniftry in that part of the town now called
the firft fociety; and the fame having been fo
appropriated and applied in manner aforefaid,

it

1786.

Hunting-
ton, &c.
againft
Carpenter

Hunting-
ton, &c.
against
Carpenter.

it ought to be confidered as an appropriation or fequeftration to that ufe, according to the ancient ufage and practice, and fo is confirmed by the ftatute in fuch cafe provided, (vid. ftat. book, 159.)—So judgement was for the defendant, as he held by leafe from the firft fociety in faid Norwich; and faid firft fociety were adjudged to hold the lands in exclufion of the town at large.

The *Chief Juftice* faid, he was doubtful whether all the reafons affigned by the court were conclufive; but on the 3d there could be no doubt, it being a point fully fettled by former adjudications.

Note.——Judge *Dyer* did not fit in this cafe, being uncle to one of the plaintiffs; and Judge *Ellfworth* excufed himfelf, having at a former trial been of counfel for the defendant.

AVERY *againft* WITMORE—*(Sheriff.)*

If a sheriff be attached in a civil fuit, the procefs is abateable.

THIS action was inftituted againft the fheriff, for the default of one of his deputies, by writ of attachment, and the fheriff's body arrefted.—He pleaded in abatement, that during his continuance in the office of fheriff, his perfon was not liable to arreft or imprifonment, by civil procefs; and for caufe alledged, that as the fheriff is ex officio keeper of the prifon, an imprifonment of his perfon would operate as a releafe to the prifoners of the county.——On the plea of abatement, the cafe was appealed to the fuperior court—and for the reafon alledged in the plea the procefs abated.

It was then contended on the part of the plaintiff, that the *fuit* ought to proceed as a *fummon,*
and

and to ceaſe only in its operation againſt the perſon of the ſheriff. But *the Court* ſaid, that the mode of proceſs being improper, it muſt abate, in toto.

Note—The ſubſtance of this Report was given me by **Mr.** *Huntington.*

N. B. *It is the practice of all courts in the ſtate of Connecticut, to try pleas in abatement with-out any anſwer. If the plaintiff chooſes, he may demur on traverſe, but if he does not chooſe, he in-forms the court, ore tenus, what parts of the plea he denies, and the court direct an enquiry; but otherwiſe, it ſtands demurred to, and the record is,* " *plea in abatement ſufficient, or inſufficient.*"

Note.——In this county, March term, 1784, the court eſtabliſhed a ſtanding rule for computing intereſt on obliga-tions, where one or more payments have been made——Which follows—Compute the intereſt to the time of the firſt payment; if that be one year or more from the time the intereſt commenced; add it to the principal, and de-duct the payment from the ſum total. If there be after pay-ments made, compute the intereſt on the balance due to the next payment, and then deduct the payment as above; and in like manner from one payment to another, till all the payments are abſorbed; provided the time between one pay-ment and another be one year or more.——But if any pay-ment be made before one year's intereſt hath accrued, then compute the intereſt on the principal ſum due on the obli-gation for one year, add it to the principal, and compute the intereſt on the ſum paid, from the time it was paid, up to the end of the year; add it to the ſum paid, and deduct that ſum from the principal and intereſt added as above. If any payments be made of a leſs ſum than the intereſt ari-ſen at the time of ſuch payment, no intereſt is to be com-puted but only on the principal ſum for any period.

C HENSHAW

1786.

HENSHAW *againſt* CURTIS COE *and* JOSEPH
COE, *Executors of* JOSEPH COE, *deceaſed.*

ERROR from the court of common pleas.
——*Henſhaw* brought his action on the
caſe againſt the defendants.—The declaration
contained two counts—

1. That in November, 1769, one *Eliſha Clark*
(ſince dead) executed a promiſſory note to the
teſtator for eighteen pounds ten ſhillings. And
in Auguſt, 1771, for the conſideration of twenty pounds eight ſhillings and nine pence (being
the principal and intereſt then due) the *teſtator*
aſſigned it to the plaintiff.—That the plaintiff
had demanded payment of *Clark*, who refuſed,
of which he had given notice to the *teſtator*;
whereupon he became liable, aſſumed, &c.

2. Count for money had and received.

The defendants pleaded to the firſt count,—
That having prayed oyer of the note, there appeared to be endorſed on the back thereof by
the plaintiff, ſix pounds twelve ſhillings and ſixpence; received of ſaid *Clark*, in January, 1779;
and in April, 1780, judgement was rendered for
the remainder.—That at the time of the aſſignment of ſaid note to the plaintiff, and for ſeveral years after, ſaid *Clark* was abundantly able
to diſcharge the debt.—That the plaintiff did
not proſecute ſaid note in the law, until more
than eight years after he received it; nor did
he within that time give any notice to the *teſtator*, or the defendants, that ſaid *Clark* had refuſed payment; but held the ſame in his own
cuſtody, without offering to return it; that ſaid
Clark is now dead, inſolvent, and the contents
of ſaid note loſt.

That the ſecond count is for the ſame matter,
cauſe and thing alledged in the firſt count.

The plaintiff demurred generally—and judgement was rendered for the defendants.

The error aſſigned was, that the plea in bar was in ſubſtance the general iſſue, and contained only a denial of the facts ſtated in the declaration; therefore could not be pleaded in bar, but if true, ought to have been given in evidence under the general iſſue.

Mr. *Dana* and Mr. *Woodruff*, for the defendants in error, pleaded in abatement, that the plaintiff appealed from the judgement of the court of common pleas during the ſitting of the court, and entered bonds therefor, according to law; therefore final judgement was not yet rendered in ſaid cauſe.

Mr. *Miller*, for the plaintiff in error, demurred, becauſe no duty had been paid on the appeal—and the plea was adjudged inſufficient.

BY THE WHOLE COURT.——The appeal was void, the ſtate duty not having been paid and certified as the law directs; therefore no proceſs was pending thereon.——The defendants then pleaded *in nullo eſt erratum*—and the judgment of the court of common pleas was affirmed.

BY THE WHOLE COURT.——By the aſſignment of the note declared upon, the plaintiff was fully empowered to recover and receive the money due thereon, of *Eliſha Clark*, who executed the note : And therefore the defendants could not be liable to any action thereon, unleſs the plaintiff ſhould ſhow that the money could not be recovered or obtained from *Clark*, either on account of its *not being due*, or the *promiſſor* being *inſolvent* at the *time* of the *aſſignment*, or ſome act of the aſſignor to *diſcharge it afterwards* : Neither of which is alledged in the preſent caſe. And *Clark*, years after the aſſignment, became and is inſolvent. And the plaintiff, by receiving part of the money due on the note of the promiſſor, is conſidered in law as accepting him payor for the whole.

The State *againſt* Luther Stutson.

Aiding in the act of counterfeiting, is within both the letter and reaſon of the ſtatute, as much as aſſiſting in making the implements.

STUTSON was indicted on the ſtatute againſt counterfeiting, and a verdict found againſt him.—The indictment charged, that he did feloniouſly *aid and aſſiſt Bazaleel Phelps*, in making and counterfeiting *fifteen French guineas*, one hundred *Spaniſh milled dollars*, and one hundred *piſtareens*, of falſe and baſe metal, in likeneſs and imitation of the true guineas, &c.——
The words of the ſtatute are, " That whoſoever
" ſhall ſtamp, or any other ways counterfeit any
" of the coins of gold or ſilver currently paſſing
" in this ſtate, or that ſhall utter and put off any
" ſuch counterfeit coins, knowing the ſame to
" be baſe, falſe and counterfeit, or that ſhall
" make any inſtrument or inſtruments, for the
" counterfeiting any of the coins aforeſaid, or
" ſhall be aiding and aſſiſting therein," &c.

Mr. *Root*, of counſel for the priſoner, moved in arreſt, and for cauſe alledged, that the offence charged is not provided againſt by ſtatute.

The motion was over-ruled——For,

By the whole Court.——The exception under the motion is, that the *aiding and aſſiſting* in the ſtatute, is limited to that of making the implements for counterfeiting, and extends not to that of counterfeiting itſelf, which is the aiding and aſſiſting laid in the indictment.

Both the letter and the reaſon of the ſtatute extend to aiding and aſſiſting in the latter caſe, as well as the former: And beſides, whoever does in fact aſſiſt in the counterfeiting, does a part of it, and is as truly the counterfeiter as any one can be who does not execute the whole alone; and it is immaterial whether he be charged as a ſole or joint agent in the matter.—So that the allegation that he did *aſſiſt* in the counterfeiting,

1786.

terfeiting, is fubftantially the fame as that he did counterfeit, &c? and brings him fully within the ftatute as a principal.

Philip Mortimer, *Efq. againft* Charles *and* George Caldwell.

A partner-ship is dif-folved, and all company effects af-figned to one partner; who be-comes bound to pay the company debts: He becomes a bankrupt, a fpecial act of infolvency is paffed in his favour, exempting his body from impri-fonment up-on his af-figning his property to truftees for the ufe of his creditors. He complies with the pro-vifion in the act, and af-figns the company property: The compa-ny debts are exhibited to his truftees, and avera-ged among his private debts;—-the other part-ner is ftill liable to pay the remain-der due on company debts.

ACTION on book debt.——The defendants pleaded, that the book of the plaintiff, on oyer, is found to confift of articles and fervices done and furnifhed for the defendants, as co-partners and traders in company, between the years 1761 and 1766.—That on the 15th day of December, 1768, the defendants, by a wri-ting under their hands, diffolved the co-part-nerfhip of the company of *Charles* and *George Caldwell.*—And by the fame writing, the faid *Charles* affigned over and conveyed to faid *George,* all the company concerns, intereft and credits, for faid *George,* to receive and convert to his own ufe.—And *George,* in confideration thereof, took upon himfelf, covenanted and en-gaged, to pay all the company debts then due: And thereby, all the company intereft and cre-dits, became the property of faid *George,* and it became his duty to pay and difcharge all the company debts.—That the book on which, &c. is one of faid company debts, which it was the duty of faid *George* to pay and fatisfy.—That faid *Charles* being divefted of all property or right to the company dues, intereft and credits, and faid *George* being reduced by loffes and mif-fortunes, preferred his petition to the General Affembly in May, 1771, reprefenting his loffes, misfortunes, and inability to pay all faid debts. The

The Gen. Aſſembly inquired into the matter, and found that his debts, including ſaid company debts, which it was his duty to pay, amounted to 5,788*l.* 9*s.* 4¼*d.* and that his eſtate and credits amounted to 3,049*l.* 0*s.* 9¼*d.* including ſaid company intereſts and credits.—That the General Aſſembly paſſed a ſpecial act of inſolvency, exempting the perſon of ſaid *George* from impriſonment from any debt then due, upon aſſigning over all his property as before ſtated, to truſtees therein mentioned, for the uſe of his creditors.—*(Which act is recited at large in the plea.)*

That ſaid *George* did, in purſuance and compliance with ſaid act of Aſſembly, make over and aſſign to ſaid truſtees all his eſtate, both real and perſonal, with all the eſtate, dues, and credits of ſaid company of *Charles* and *George Caldwell,* to and for the uſe and benefit of his creditors.—And that they ever have been ſince, at the ſole diſpoſal and direction of ſaid creditors, one of whom was the plaintiff, who was privy to, and acquieſced in ſaid tranſaction.

That in May, 1772, upon application of ſaid truſtees, the General Aſſembly, by a ſpecial act, empowered them to ſue for, and recover all the debts, credits and monies due to ſaid *George,* and the late company of *Charles* and *George,* and when recovered, to divide and diſtribute the ſame amongſt his creditors.—*(Which act is recited at large in the plea.)*

And that thereupon all the eſtate, intereſts, ſecurities, papers, vouchers, and receipts, relating to ſaid company debts and credits, were delivered over into the hands of ſaid truſtees to ſettle and adjuſt with the ſeveral creditors, and ſaid *Charles* and *George* are wholly diveſted of them, and have no means in their power to evince any payments that have been made;
and

and thereupon ſaid *George Caldwell*, and ſaid company of *Charles* and *George Caldwell*, became exonerated and diſcharged from all ſuits and demands againſt them, for any debts due and owing from ſaid company, until a final average ſhould be made out by ſaid truſtees, purſuant to ſaid act of inſolvency; and then only for the reſiduum of ſaid debts that ſhould be found due after ſuch average ſhould be made.—And that no average hath been made out by ſaid truſtees, but the ſame is ſtill depending in the hands of ſaid truſtees, ſubject, as it ever has been, to the order and direction of ſaid creditors, of whom the ſaid *Philip Mortimer* was, and is one.

To this there was a demurrer, and joinder in demurrer.

By the Court.——The plea is inſufficient. —The ſpecial act of inſolvency ſet forth in the plea, goes to the exemption of the perſon of *George*, one of the defendants (leaving his eſtate liable, which he may afterwards acquire.) But it extends not to *Charles*, the other defendant. He is not named in it. Nor is it grounded on any ſuppoſed inability of his, to pay the company debts. Nor does it operate to diſcharge him on the ground of the ſuppoſed hardſhip there would be in his remaining liable, after the perſon of the other joint debtor is liberated, and the company effects and papers are gone into the hands of truſtees and out of his controul. If he is in fact more expoſed and defenceleſs to his creditors, ſince the paſſing the act of inſolvency, than he was before, it does not follow that it has diſcharged him. But he ever was liable to be levied upon, ſolely, for all the company debts, and all their contracts were, in their nature, joint and ſeveral. Nor is it owing to the paſſing of the act of inſolvency,

that

that he has not right to controul the company effects; he having ſold and relinquiſhed his ſhare
in them years before, at the diſſolution of the
partnerſhip; and the act provides for no other
aſſignment than of that which is conſidered as
George's eſtate. Nor need there be any diffi-
culty about the company books, and papers.
Free acceſs may be had to them, and an order
of court, if neceſſary, might be obtained for their
being brought into court when requiſite in the
trial of a cauſe.

If the truſtees have paid the plaintiff any part
of his debt, out of the avails of the effects, aſſigned to them, it can be ſhown and applied
when damages come to be aſſeſſed. A balance,
it is clear, there muſt be due to him, even if the
aſſignment to the truſtees be conſidered as an
actual payment to the creditors, and to the nominal amount of the credits and effects aſſigned. And no reaſon appears why judgement
ſhould not be rendered in the preſent action,
for the aſcertaining and recovering what ſtill
remains due.

Judge DYER,—*diſſenting.*—*C.* and *G. Cald-*
well, when they entered into contract with the
plaintiff, were known to be in company; and
every contract they made muſt be conſidered
and governed by the true legal intention of the
parties, and the laws of the ſtate then in being
and force; and if altered by any *poſt facto* law,
or private act of the legiſlature, will operate to
deſtroy or render void the original contract.
Bacon's Abr. tit. *ſtatute* c.—*Salkeld* 198—*Brew-*
ſter vs. *Kitchel.*—But it cannot operate to ſubject the obligors, their perſons or eſtate, in a
different manner from what they were obliged at the time of the contract. On a bond,
A and *B* are joint obligors; if the name or ſeal
of one is taken off, it is deſtroyed as to the other.

Charles

. *Charles* and *George*, and each of them, at the time of contracting with the plaintiff, knew and confidered that the body and eftate of each were pledged for the fatisfaction, or to compel the payment of the debt: And *Charles* muft confider, that the body of his brother *George* was liable to be taken and holden to compel him to turn out or produce his eftate (if any) for the fatisfaction of the debt, as well as his own :— This alfo the plaintiff well knew, and was the legal fecurity he depended upon. If the Affembly, by a fovereign act, and of a private nature, have undertaken to liberate the perfon of *George* from being liable to be taken and holden to compel him to produce his eftate, (if any) it materially alters the original contract and fecurity, both as to debtors and creditors.—And the creditor, by confenting thereto (without which the act could not operate to the difadvantage of *Charles*, the other partner) does as effectually difcharge the original contract, as if by his own immediate act, he had difcharged one of the joint debtors.—In the prefent cafe, if judgement is rendered in favour of the plaintiff, he cannot take the body of *George*—*George* may poffefs large property, which can eafily be kept out of the way of the creditor's execution ; and his body being exempt, there is no way to compel a difcovery : (For that is the only folid ground or reafon of the law fubjecting the body to be taken.) Now the body of *George* being liberated, it neceffarily' cafts the whole upon *Charles*, effentially different from the original contract. It is objected, that on the original contract, the creditor, if he pleafed, might collect the whole out of the eftate of either, or take the body of either without the other, and compel him to produce eftate to pay the whole.— True it is fo ; but then *Charles* had an equal

H   chance

Mortimer
againſt
Caldwell.

chance with *George*, that *George* might be compelled to pay the whole, or at leaſt the one half:
But if the act in favour of *George* is operative,
in this caſe, it exempts *George*, and neceſſarily
caſts the whole upon *Charles*, contrary to the
legal underſtanding and operation of the original contract.

It is further objected, that it appears from
the law authorities, that by the operation of the
bankrupt laws in England, where one partner
becomes a bankrupt, the other is notwithſtanding ſubjected to all intents and purpoſes, as
though his partner had taken no benefit thereby.—To which I anſwer, that the ſtatute reſpecting bankrupts in England, is a general ſub-
ſiſting law of the kingdom, antecedent to all
debts or contracts, which are affected by it.
Therefore, when a contract is made, (a general
public law exiſting) ſuch contract muſt be conſidered by the contracting parties, and underſtood as ſubject to ſuch law. This is what I
contend for.—The act now pleaded, exempting
the body of *George*, is a private act, which did
not exiſt at the time this debt was contracted,
but was made long ſince; therefore could not
be had in conſideration by the parties contracting: But the laws then exiſting, ſubjected the
bodies of both to be taken, and held to compel
a ſatisfaction of the debt; one of which is ſince
liberated by this act: The plaintiff and the other
creditors, have conformed themſelves thereto;
which eſſentially alters the original contract.

Another point of ſome weight and conſideration in the caſe is, that the company debts and
intereſts were all made over to *George*, and with
the eſtate of *George*, by act of law and the creditors, was made over to commiſſioners appointed by the creditors, and the plaintiff in particular: And which commiſſioners are appointed
and

and empowered to examine all debts and demands againſt ſaid company, and aſcertain the ſums due, and, to apportion out to the ſeveral creditors their ſeveral parts, as in caſe of inſolvent eſtates, &c.—and that the ſame ſtill lies before the commiſſioners unfiniſhed.—I am, therefore, of opinion, the action does not at preſent lie before the courts of common law to aſcertain the debt of any creditor, but before the commiſſioners: Neither can any certain judgement be rendered by this court in the preſent caſe, as the commiſſioners have not determined what is the plaintiff's proportion of the eſtate in their hands.

Upon the whole, it appears unjuſt, and not conſonant to reaſon or equity, that on a joint or company contract of *George* and *Charles* Caldwell, a judgement ſhould be rendered which will ſubject the body of *Charles* to be taken and impriſoned, at the pleaſure of a creditor, tho' no eſtate in his hands, when at the ſame time *George* may have a plentiful eſtate, but his body liberated, and no means left either for *Charles* himſelf, the plaintiff or any other creditor, to compel *George* to diſcover or produce his eſtate for the ſatisfaction of the company debts, or any part thereof, but *Charles* alone is ſubjected, contrary to his original contract and undertaking.

WOODRUFF *against* WHITTLESEY.

Trover for a
heifer. The
plaintiff
claimed said
heifer by a
transfer f om
Nathaniel B.
Woodruff:
The defend-
ant alledged
the transfer
was fraudu-
lent, and on
this point
rested his de-
fence.

THIS was an action of trover for a heifer.—
Plea, Not guilty.—The plaintiff claim-
ed the property of the heifer, by a transfer from
Nathaniel Baldwin Woodruff, on the 24th day of
October, 1783, in payment of a debt due to the
plaintiff by note. Two witnesses testified to the
sale: They said it was in the evening—that they
were only called in to witness the bill of sale,
which was written in another room,—They did
not see any note delivered up, but understood
from the conversation, which then passed between *Baldwin Woodruff* and the plaintiff, that
a certain debt, due by note, was the consideration of the bill of sale.

The only question was, whether the transfer
from *Baldwin Woodruff* to the plaintiff, was fraudulent. The defendant, *Whittlesey*, was a constable, and at the suit of one *Murray*, attached
the heifer in question, the 18th day of November, '83, as the property of *Baldwin Woodruff*. It
was proved by the defendant, that the possession
of the heifer, after the pretended transfer to the
plaintiff, was not changed, till taken by the defendant.—That the bill of sale, by which the
plaintiff claimed, was dated one day before
Baldwin Woodruff had acquired any property in
the heifer; and he had frequently said, he never would pay *Murray* any thing, but would put
his estate out of his hands to avoid it (though
it was at that time only a right of action.)

These circumstances were urged by the defendant as so many indisputable badges of fraud,
to which was cited, 2 *Wilson's Reports*, 260—
3 *Coke*, 82, *Twine's* case.—1 *Burrow*, 467, *Worse-
ley, & al.* vs. *De Mattos* and *Slader*—2 *Burrow*, 831, *Wilson* vs. *Day*—*Cowper's Reports*, 434.
The

The jury found a verdict for the defendant, which was accepted by the whole court.

Woodruff
againſt
Whittleſey

The plaintiff's counſel then moved in arreſt of judgement, and for cauſe alledged,—

1. That on trial of ſaid cauſe before the court and jury, the only queſtion was, whether the tranſaction between *Solomon Woodruff*, the plaintiff, and *Nathaniel B. Woodruff*, on the 24th day of October, 1783, relative to the ſale of ſaid heifer, was fraudulent, as it reſpected a demand of one *Philemon Murray*, upon ſaid *Nathaniel B. Woodruff*. And that in evidence, the defendant exhibited a writ of attachment, in favour of ſaid *Murray*, againſt ſaid *Baldwin Woodruff*, in an action for *ſlander*, demanding forty ſhillings damages; which writ was dated the 7th day of October, and ſerved the 18th day of November, 1783. And that ſaid writ of attachment, and judgement thereon, was the only evidence of any debt, on the part of ſaid *Murray*, againſt ſaid *Baldwin Woodruff*, which could not be conſidered as a debt, until after ſaid 18th day of November; therefore, at the time of ſaid bargain and ſale of ſaid heifer, from ſaid *Baldwin Woodruff* to the plaintiff, there was no certain claim, debt or demand exiſting, on the part of ſaid *Murray*, againſt ſaid *Baldwin Woodruff*, ſo as to make ſaid ſale fraudulent.

2. That one of the jurors who tried ſaid cauſe, had previouſly to ſaid trial given his opinion in ſaid cauſe.

The motion was over-ruled.

BY THE WHOLE COURT.—The firſt exception is inſufficient; becauſe the court, on motion in arreſt, after a general verdict of the jury, cannot reſort back to the evidence on which the verdict was founded, to ſet it aſide, but muſt render judgement according to the facts found.

The court will never reſort to the evidence on which a verdict is founded, as a ground of arreſt, but will conſider as concluſive, the facts found by the verdict.

And

1786.

And, upon examination into the facts alledged in the second exception, it does not appear that there was any partiality in the juror, who is said to have given his opinion in the cafe, before the trial, as he declares he had no remembrance of it; and, although it was teltified by two young men that they had heard him, some years ago, give his opinion in a tranfient difcourfe, yet it doth not appear that that opinion was founded on a full knowledge of the cafe, or that it had any influence on his mind in the trial. And it was further fhown, that the other jurors were very unanimous in giving their verdict as they did, before they had heard his opinion.

A party to a fraudulent conveyance, and not a party in the fuit, cannot be a witnefs, nor is what he has faid, when the party fued was not prefent, admiffible.

NOTE.—*In this cafe it was moved, on the part of the defendant, that he might introduce teftimony of what Baldwin Woodruff had acknowledged, as to the fraud in faid fale.*———But, *record, that*

BY THE COURT.———*What a perfon hath been heard to fay, who is only interefted in the event of a fuit, but not a party to it, cannot be given in evidence; for though a perfon may confefs for himfelf, he cannot for another.*

It was alfo moved to enquire the character of the parties to the fraudulent conveyance, as to honefty—which was over-ruled by the court.

WHOLE COURT.———The complaint

BILL *againft* SCOTT.

When a juftice of the peace binds to good behaviour, he can bind only till the next court of common pleas, leaving it to the difcretion of that court to continue or difcharge the bonds.

ERROR from the judgement of a Juftice of the Peace.———Scott brought his action qui tam, againft Bill for an affault and battery, demanding damage four pounds.—The Juftice rendered judgement for the plaintiff, which was

recorded in thefe words :—— " Watertown,
" January 28th 1786.——At a court for the trial
" of fmall caufes, *Thomas Fenn*, Efq. Juftice of
" the Peace for Litchfield county, prefent ;—
" *Elijah Bill*, of Watertown, was brought by a
" fpecialty to anfwer to a complaint figned by
" *Eliphaz Scott*, of faid Watertown, for breach
" of the peace. The court opened,—the delin-
" quent, in court, pleaded, Not guilty. The
" plaintiff teftified, under oath, that he was guil-
" ty; and evidence was fworn, examined, and
" the cafe heard at large.——This court find
" damage for the plaintiff 4l. lawful money,
" and 10s. fine to the public, and order faid
" *Elijah Bill* to find fufficient bond of 100l. for
" his peaceable behaviour, and to pay coft, tax-
" ed at 19s. 9d."

Errors affigned,—1. That it appears from the
record, that the teftimony of the plaintiff in
the action was admitted on the trial; which was
illegal.

2. That the bond for the good behaviour of
the then defendant, was illegally taken, for that
no time is fet when it may expire, nor any reference had to any court where the plaintiff can
obtain relief againft it.

And without argument, the judgement of the
Juftice was reverfed.——For,

By the whole Court.——The complain-
ant who profecuted, as well for his own damages
as for a breach of the peace, was admitted as a
witnefs in the cafe—which was illegal.

And it doth not appear from the record, that
the defendant was found guilty, though he was
adjudged to pay damages and cofts.

The defendant was bound to his good behaviour, without day, or reference to any court:
Whereas, a Juftice of the Peace can bind, in
fuch cafe, only to the next court of common
pleas,

1786.

pleas, leaving it to the difcretion of that court to continue or difcharge the bonds.

A CTION on the cafe for words, &c. the plaintiff in his declaration, as attorney at law.

The declaration concluded with thefe words—"That by reafon of the fpeaking, uttering and publifhing the falfe and fcandal...

THIS was an action of trefpafs for cutting timber.—The defendant pleaded the general iffue.——The principal point in difpute was, the validity of a quit-claim deed from the plaintiff to the defendant, under which the defendant claimed title.

The cafe was, in 1784, an action of trefpafs was pending between the fame parties for cutting on the lands now in queftion, with claims ...ing. The controverfy was fubmitted to arbitration. Quit-claim deeds from each to the other were executed, acknowledged, and delivered into the hands of the arbitrators, to be by them difpofed of as they fhould award the title. The arbitrators, upon hearing, awarded the title to be in *Goodwin*, the defendant, and delivered to him the deeds. There was fome contention at the trial, whether *Peck* did not forbid the delivery of the deed after the arbitrators had publifhed their award: But *the Court* faid it was immaterial, for the publifhing the award was the condition of the delivery; that being performed, the deed became abfolute. And although the fee of lands cannot be transferred by award of arbitrators, yet it may well be done by deed, as in this cafe.

The jury rendered a verdict for the defendant, which was approved by the whole court.

BOSTWICK

BOSTWICK *against* NICKELSON.

ACTION on the cafe for words, refpecting the plaintiff in his profeffion, as attorney at law.

The declaration concluded with thefe words :—" That by reafon of the defendant's uttering " and publifhing the falfe and fcandalous words " aforefaid, thofe who ufed to employ him in " their cafes and important concerns, daily " withdraw themfelves, their bufinefs," &c.

The defendant's council fuggefted to the court, that the plaintiff had alledged fpecial damage; and therefore moved to enquire whether any had been fuftained.

Mr. *Reeve*, counfel for the plaintiff, denied that thofe words in the declaration mounted to an allegation of fpecial damage; and cited the cafe of *Browning* vs. *Newman*, 1 *Strange*, 666; alfo *Buller's Nifi Prius*, 7th *page*.

BY THE COURT.——This declaration is general; there are no damages fo particularly fet forth, as to ground a fpecial enquiry.

In an action of flander, evidence shall not be given of special damage, unless it be alledged in the declaration.

STODDARD *against* BIRD.

ACTION of trefpafs for falfe imprifonment.——The declaration ftates, that, " On " the 26th day of September, A. D. 1785, in " the northeaft precinct, in Dutchefs county, " ftate of New-York, (within the county of Litch- " field) with force and arms, a high handed af- " fault on the body of the plaintiff the defendant " did make, and did then and there, without " law or right, in a fpiteful and malicious man- " ner,

Action for falfe imprifonment may be maintained, where one procures procefs without caufe of action, & caufes another to be arrefted with defign to extort money from him without any legal or equitable foundation.

I

"ner, take, feize, and caufe to be arrefted, the
"body of the plaintiff, and with the fame force
"and arms him did unlawfully, wrongfully, and
"falfly imprifon, hold, abufe and reftrain from
"his liberty for the fpace of three days, until he
"did make, caufe and compel the plaintiff to
"pay large fums of money, in order to obtain
"his liberty, &c.

The general iffue being pleaded, the cafe appeared to be thus :—The plaintiff was adminni-
ftrator on the eftate of *Jofiah Stoddard*, deceafed : He had made a reprefentation of infolvency to the court of probate for the diftrict of
Sharon ; commiffioners had been appointed,
who received and examined the claims exhibited againft the eftate, and had reported the fame
to be infolvent. No average had been made to
the creditors, or ordered to be made by the
court of probate, but was ftill pending. The
defendant had exhibited a debt of thirty-fix fhillings lawful money againft faid eftate, to the
commiffioners, previoufly to the imprifonment
complained of, which was allowed.—While
thefe matters were thus pending before the court
of probate, the plaintiff being in the ftate of
New-York, the defendant there applied to a
Juftice of the Peace, and prayed out a *capias*
againft the perfon of the plaintiff, for the fame
debt of thirty fhillings, which had been exhibited to the commiffioners, as a claim againft the
eftate of *Stoddard*, deceafed.—The plaintiff was
taken by virtue of this writ, carried before the
Juftice, there held in cuftody till he procured
fpecial bail, and was held to a trial ; on which,
judgement was rendered againft him for debt
and coft.

It was not agreed by the parties, nor did it
appear on trial, whether the procefs iffued by
the Juftice was regular, and confiftent with the
laws of the ftate of New-York.

Mr. *Reeve* and Mr. *Tracy*, for the plaintiff, urged that *Luther Stoddard*, the plaintiff, was not liable, by the laws of Connecticut, to any kind of suit for the debt which *Bird* had exhibited to the commissioners, during its pendency, before the court of probate. The procefs issued by the Justice was illegal, and not warranted by the laws of the state of New-York; for the claufe, *ac etiam billæ*, could not legally be inferted. The British statute of the 13. Car. 2, which prohibits the inferting of that claufe, against executors and administrators, has been explicitly adopted by the state of New-York. But admitting the form of the writ to have been regular, *Stoddard* ought not to have been arrested; the usual return of common bail only should have been made. Therefore, the fuit being groundlefs in the first instance, and illegal in the procefs and execution, the defendant who procured it, with a wicked intention, was guilty of a trefpafs, and must be liable to refpond in damages.

Mr. *Root* and Mr. *Canfield*, for the defendant, admitted the laws of this state as urged on the other fide, but denied that by the laws of the state of New-York any other form or procefs could have been issued, than the one issued by the Justice. If special bail was not required by law in cafe of an administrator, the officer did wrong not to make return of common bail and dismifs *Stoddard*: But this would be the wrong doing of the officer, and not of *Bird*, the defendant. If the writ legally issued, no action of falfe imprifonment can be fustained against *Bird* for the act of the officer.

If there was any informality in the writ, or if the action was not fuftainable before the Justice, *Stoddard* has waved all advantages which he might have derived from that quarter, by not

pleading

pleading in abatement at that time. As he
pleaded to the merits, he acknowledged the jurisdiction, and admitted the legality of the process, and the judgement being rendered against
him on that issue, it is to be presumed that the
right of action was well supported, according to
the laws of that state. Lord *Raymond*, 229.
The febt vs. *Carpenter* and *Munn*. The present action is entirely immaterial whether. If
Stoddard has any right of action, it must be *case*,
and not *trespass*, and not return any cause of
action. The jury found a verdict for the plaintiff,
on which the court delivered the following opinions: that state; and the presumption is
that *Judge* Ellsworth. Right of action against
an administrator, is transitory, and the action
may be brought wherever he is found. And
though he is not to be arrested according to the
mode of process in this state, he may be, for
ought appears in the state of New-York. And
the presumption is he may, because the authority there issued a warrant to make the arrest,
and held him to trial upon it.

As to the suit *there*, being without cause, and
vexatious; this is not to be intended, but the
contrary, after a judgement in the plaintiff's favour, on a full trial upon the merits; but if it
was so, yet if the arrest and holding was by a
lawful precept, an action of false imprisonment
is not the proper remedy, but an action on the
case, or upon the statute against vexatious suits.
I think no trespass is here proved; and therefore that the jury have found wrong.

Judge Birds. As it appears that the administrator conducted properly, he ought to be
protected, otherwise no person would be safe in
that situation. The laws of this state undoubtedly protect administrators from arrests, on account of the deceased whom they represent. For
if

1786.

Stoddard
against
Bird

if it was otherwise, and they might be legally
arrested in this way, whenever they should hap-
pen to go out of the state, they would be liable
to be punished. Therefore I think the process was
illegal, and the suit unwarrantable. In no mind
of Judge Sherman.—Undoubtedly there are
instances where one may make use of legal authority in such manner as to become liable to
the action of false imprisonment. As where one
will arrest another by legal authority, without
any cause of action, and not return the writ, &c.
But in this case it does not appear but the suit
was legally instituted agreeably to the forms of
that state; and the presumption is rather that
way, for the action went to trial, and judgement
was rendered by court and jury against the present plaintiff. I think that so far justifies the
transaction, that this kind of remedy is not applicable to the supposed injury. I am therefore
of opinion the jury are wrong.

Judge Drake.—Every cause will have its
own peculiar complexion and leading cast. The
facts here are conceded. The action of false
imprisonment always goes on this ground,—is
the imprisonment complained of right, or is it
wrong? If it appears to have been right, the
action fails; if wrong, the action is supportable.
View the complexion of this case. It appears
that Bird, the defendant, designed to extort
from the plaintiff, in this way, a sum of money
which he could not recover by law, and which
Stoddard was not bound by justice to pay. I
this is abusing the law. Perhaps there may be
another remedy for the injury; but I think that
does not bar this suit. It is clear that Bird had
no right in this state to arrest Stoddard, or even
summon him before a court of justice, for the
debt, under the circumstances which then attended it. I think he had no right to do it at all.

But

One may
make use of
legal autho-
rity in such
manner as to
become lia-
ble to an ac-
tion for false
imprison-
ment.

1786.

Stoddard against Bird.

But there was a writ taken out to arrest the body of *Stoddard*. Did he mean to have such a writ? He undoubtedly did, for no other would answer his purpose. The intention and design, then, was wrongful, and the act injurious; so that I cannot see but the jury have done right.

LAW, *Chief Justice.*——So far seems to be agreed, that the defendant has done wrong. The only question is, whether the plaintiff has chosen his proper and legal remedy. There are many cases where a man may have two remedies for the same injury : He may then make his election which he will pursue. The law means that a remedy shall be provided for every wrong, that will do equal justice to both the parties. Will this action do compleat justice? I am not certain but it will do as ample justice as any other.——There is no evidence but that the defendant applied for just such a writ as was issued ; and it is most reasonable to suppose that he did, and that the officer conducted rightly, and agreeably to the precept. The plaintiff has consequently been injured by the procurement and wrong act of the defendant. I am therefore of opinion the verdict is right.

It was accordingly established.

BENEDICT *against* BROWNSON.

A witness is not admissible where he has a promise to receive part of the avails of the suit; though, if the party was indebted to him, and had no visible means of payment but by recovery, that alone would not exclude him.

IN this case the plaintiff offered a witness, who had engaged to pay his, the plaintiff's, attorney for carrying on the suit (the plaintiff being a poor man) and had a promise from the plaintiff that part of the avails of the suit, if a recovery was had, should be applied to the pay-

ment of a debt then due to the witness from the
plaintiff.

...He is interested and inadmissible, as he bases a promise to share the benefit of the recovery, if he had. Though, if the objection went no further than, that the plaintiff was indebted to him, and had no visible means of payment, excepting by a recovery, it would not exclude him. That point has been long decided.

WARNER against PHELPS.

THIS was an action of book debt. The account exhibited consisted of one article only, (to wit) twenty half-johannes. The charge was not in the hand writing of the deceased.

Mr. *Adams*, for the defendant, moved, that the plaintiff be compelled to produce the original entries of the deceased, or suffer a *non-suit*.

Mr. *Hinman*, for the plaintiff, stated, that by accident, the original entries, which were in the hand writing of the deceased, were totally lost, and could not be produced—That the account exhibited was made by the attorney, in consequence of directions received from the deceased, in his life time—That the plaintiff could prove there had been a charge in the hand writing of the deceased, exactly corresponding with the one exhibited on trial, and that the deceased had declared the same to be a just charge.

Mr. *Adams*, in reply, said, that if administrators were permitted to sustain actions on accounts made by them in favour of the deceased, from such

In an action of book debt brought by an administrator, original entries of the deceased are not absolutely necessary to support the action.

1787.

Leavenfw.
againſt
Phelps.

fuch informatioñ as they might be able to collect, their would be no guarding againſt unjuſt
demands of this kind: For if the original papers
were produced, it might appear from them that
the account had been fettled, or that the articles
were delivered in difcharge of fome antecedent
demand; or much other light might be reflect-
ed on the fubject. That an original entry was
a fpecies of evidence indifpenfibly neceffary to
fupport a demand of this kind.

By THE COURT.——The action may proceed without thofe entries; for if the demand,
under all the circumſtances of it, fhould not be
fufficiently fupported by evidence, the action
muſt fail. The charge in the hand writing of
the deceafed, can only be evidential of a right
of recovery, which may be fupplied by other
evidence, of as great or greater weight.

M'DONALD and Others againſt LEACH.

A deed re-
ceived by a
town clerk,
to be recor-
ded, and an
entry of that
kind made
upon it;
ſhall fecure a
title to the
grantee from
the day it
was fo re-
ceived,
without any
reference to
the time, in
which the
deed is re-
corded at
length.

ACTION of diffeifin:—The general iffue
pleaded.————The cafe was, that in the
year 1775, Daniel Boſtwick was negociating a
loan of money of M'Donald, of the ſtate of New-
York. In order to obtain the money, he made
a mortgage deed to M'Donald, of the land in
queſtion, carried it to the regiſter in New-Mil-
ford, where the land lay, who received the deed,
and made an entry on the back, "received for
recording." At the fame time, the regiſter
wrote a certificate directed to M'Donald, that
Boſtwick had lodged fuch a deed in his office,
which was entered on record. Boſtwick alfo
told the regiſter not to record the deed at that
time. The regiſter, accordingly wrote on the

deed below the entry first made, "not record,"
and placed the deed in a bundle of the same
kind, where it remained till about the year 1783.
Bostwick carried the certificate, which the register had given him, to M'Donald, and procured
the money. Some years after Bostwick conveyed the same land to Angus Nickelson, (there appearing to be no embarrassment to the title, on
record) and Nickelson conveyed to the defendant; both of which deeds were recorded at full
length.—Subsequent to this, M'Donald discovered that his deed had never been recorded at
full length.—He searched the office, found it,
procured it to be recorded, and then brought
his action.

Mr. Root and Mr. Reeve, for the plaintiff.—
M'Donald's deed having been lodged with the
register, and the entry made, that it was received for recording, the register was bound to
perfect the record; and no orders to the contrary, either from grantor or grantee, could go-
vern him.—By the statute respecting deeds, it
is enacted, " That no grant or deed, of bar-
" gain, sale, or mortgage, made of any houses
" or lands within this state, shall be accounted
" good and effectual in law to hold such houses
" and lands against any other person or persons
" whatsoever, but the grantor or grantors, and
" their heirs only, unless the grant or deed of
" deeds thereof, be recorded at length in the
" records of the town where such houses and lands
" ...... carried it to the register in question,
...... And the town clerk or register of every
town in this state, shall, on the receipt of any
grant, deed, conveyance, or mortgage, of any
house or land, brought to him to record, note
thereupon the day, month, and year when he
received the same, and the record shall bear
the same date." Bostwick not to record
it ..... The register accordingly wrote on the
deed

The latter clause of this statute is in some degree explanatory of the first, and shows that the entry of the register on the deed, and the lodging it in the office, is in judgement of law a recording, so far as to secure the title; and when compleated, the title by relation becomes perfect from the execution of the deed.—*See Cowper's Reports*, 705, *Doe* vs. *Routledge*—1 *Burrow*, 474, *Sir Edward Worsley*, vs. *Demattos* and *Slader*.

Mr. *Canfield* and Mr. *Everitt*, for the defendant, said, that the conduct with regard to *M'Donald's* deed had been such, that if it should be established, it would operate as a fraud upon the present defendant. He purchased when no incumbrance on *Bostwick's* title could be found on record; therefore he had the fairest grounds to presume none existed. He had pursued every legal method to authenticate his title, and ought to be secured in the enjoyment of it.—If the same care and attention had been practiced by *M'Donald*, no injustice could have taken place.

That *M'Donald's* deed, appeared not to have been delivered to the grantee at the time it was lodged in the office of the register; neither had the consideration been received: Therefore the deed was not valid, and the entries of the register were of no more consequence than those of any other person. No subsequent act of *M'Donald* could, by the doctrine of relations, restore a title which was defective in its origin.

It was observed from the *Bench*, that the Justice who took the acknowledgement, had signed himself as a witness to the *delivery*, which was an evidence of that fact, of too high a nature to be doubted.

The jury found a verdict for the plaintiff, which was accepted by the whole court.

ELDRIDGE

ELDRIDGE *against* LANE *and* ROSEVELT.

In Chancery.

THE cafe was, That on the 10th of March, A. D. 1783, the petitioner, together with one *Joʃhua Wells* and *Samuel Doud*, became obligated to *Jared Lane*, one of the refpondents, in the fum of 167*l*. 16*s*. lawful money.—*Wells* and *Doud*, in confideration that the petitioner had become bound for them, on the fame day executed to him an indemnifying bond, of fufficient amount to fave him harmlefs.—In March 1784, *Lane* put the faid obligation in fuit, and recovered a judgement for 180*l*. 4*s*. 11*d*.—The execution was levied on the petitioner's lands, and the whole contents fatisfied with his property.—In September, 1784, the petitioner recovered judgement againft *Wells* and *Doud*, on the indemnifying bond, for 203*l*. 3*s*. 4*d*. and 115*l*. 1*s*. 10*d*. on another obligation againft them.—On the 28th day of January, A. D. 1785, the petitioner caufed the executions which iffued on thofe two judgements, to be levied on a farm of land belonging to *Doud*, which on the 21ft day of June, 1777, was mortgaged by *Doud* to *Lane*, to fecure the fum of 350*l*. lawful money, and intereft, due by bond of the fame date, and payable the 20th day of June, 1779.—A payment had been made on this bond, acknowledged by a receipt in thefe words—" *Received of*
" *Mr.* Samuel Doud, *this* 14th d*dy of O*ʄt*-ber,*
" 1778, *the intereʃt of a bond given by ʃaid* ....
" *dated June* 21ʃt, 1777, *and due J*....
" 1779, *and is for the ʃum of* 350*l*. *la*....
" *likewiʃe* 250*l*. *of the principal of ʃai*....
" *ceived this day*, &c.   ....

The petitioner fuppofed at th.....

K 2

ing his executions, there was no greater lien upon the land than 100l. and the interest thereof from the 20th of June, 1779. This land was appraised to the petitioner at the sum of his two executions, under the supposed incumbrance of 100l. only. After the petitioner had compleated his levy on the land, Doud, with a design to defraud the petitioner, came to an agreement with Lane to admit there was still due on the mortgage about 400l. and to relinquish all right and title to the equity of redemption, and surrender the mortgaged land to Lane, in satisfaction of what was then due. This agreement was carried into execution by the parties, according to the forms of law.

That at the time the petitioner levied his executions on this land there was not, nor had there been at any time afterwards, any other estate of Doud or Wells, which he could obtain: And that, in all these transactions, Lane acted for Isaac Rosevelt, of the city of New-York; to whom he had conveyed, by deed of release, all his title to said lands.

It also appeared, that the payment made on the bond, and acknowledged by the receipt as lawful money, was in fact continental money, about seven eighths depreciated.

The prayer of the petition was, that Lane and Rosevelt be compelled, under a suitable penalty, to quit-claim said land to the petitioner, on payment of the sum of 100l. and the interest thereof from the 20th of June, 1779.

The court decreed, that the petitioner might redeem upon paying the amount of the mortgage monies due, deducting the payment made by Doud, at the nominal sum.

BRADLEY

BRADLEY and Others against CAMP.

ERROR from the court of common pleas, on a bill of exceptions.——The plaintiffs being trustees to the insolvent estate of *Reynold Marvin*, Esq. brought their action of book-debt against the defendant, *Joel Camp*. The general issue was pleaded and joined to the court; and a judgement rendered for the defendant.—— The case, as it appeared on trial, was then stated in a bill of exceptions, and certified by the Judge.*—Some time in the year 1759, the defendant entered into a copartnership trade with *Silas Bingham*, which extended only to the purchasing goods, from a certain Mrs. *Webb*, at Weathersfield, as occasion should require, to supply a store in Salisbury, in the county of Litchfield, for the purposes of retailing. This partnership was dissolved in May 1762, by mutual agreement. The dissolution was published, by a declaration in the hearing of several persons who were called as witnesses; and never published in any other manner, but was, however, generally known in the town of Salisbury.—By the dissolution, all debts due the company

A partnership in trade being formed, the partners are, by law, liable to be jointly charged for all credits given at the request of either partner, relating to the copartnership business; until public notice is given of a dissolution; and on a joint contract, if one only be sued, it is matter of abatement, but no advantage can be taken of it, under the general issue.

* Note.——The propriety of introducing *bills of exceptions* in this manner, has been questioned by some.—There are, however, in English books, many precedents for this practice—(vid.) *Douglass' Reports*, 363, *Blaquier* vs. *Hawkins.*—1 *Blackstone's Reports*, 555, *Money* vs. *Leach.*—*Cowper*, 161, *Mostyn* vs. *Fabrigas.* And there may, perhaps, be much more reason for adopting such a practice *here*, where many questions of law are submitted to the jury; and if a special verdict be found, no other relief can be had against an erroneous judgement: But in this case, mode of bringing it up, was not contended, and no opinion of court given upon the subject.——Since the trial of this cause, the mode of bringing up a cause by bill of exceptions, under like circumstances, has been adjudged illegal. See the case, *Fleming* against *Fisher* and *Baldwin*, reported at large.

company became the property of *Bingham*, who became obligated to pay all debts due from the company; and for that purpose gave to *Camp* a promissory note for 2800*l.* conditioned to indemnify against all demands upon the partnership. *Camp*, at the same time, received about 200*l.* for his dividend of the profits which had accrued upon their joint trade.

The account of said *Marvin*, exhibited on trial, stood charged to *Camp* and *Bingham*, in company. It contained only charges for cash advanced, and services rendered, as attorney, in prosecuting sundry suits at law, commenced in the name of *Camp* and *Bingham*, for the collection of debts which accrued to them in the course of their partnership trade.—This business was undertaken upon the application of *Bingham*, in the month of August, 1762, subsequent to the dissolution of the partnership, he being the acting partner.—*Marvin*, living in Litchfield, did not know of the partnership of *Camp* and *Bingham*, until he was requested to undertake this business; he was then told it was a company affair—which also appeared from the face of the accounts and notes to be put in suit; and he was not then notified, nor did he at any time know of the dissolution. At the same time this business was undertaken, he did business for *Bingham*, as an individual.

Camp had no knowledge that these suits were commenced, nor did he know that said *Marvin* had any demands on him or *Bingham*, for business done in their names, till a short time before the present action was instituted by the plaintiffs:—*Bingham* having the sole direction of the business done by *Marvin*, and he also received the avails thereof to his own use.

Subsequent to these transactions, and before the commencement of the present suit, *Bingham* died, a bankrupt.   On

On this cafe four queftions of law were referred to the court of common pleas :—

1. Whether the diffolution of the partnerfhip was publifhed in fuch manner as to exonerate *Camp* from the fubfequent contracts of his partner, on the company's credit.

2. Whether a diffolution of the partnerfhip, which refpected only the future purchafe and fale of goods, though it had been publifhed with all the ufual forms, could affect a contract like this, which arofe out of it, as a neceffary confequence.

3. Whether, if two or more join in fuit, it does not conftitute fuch a partnerfhip, or connection, by holding out a joint credit, as to render them all liable for the expence of profecuting, however their feveral interefts may be in the event.

4. Whether, this action being brought againft *Camp* alone, without any reference to *Bingham*, in the declaration, under all the circumftances, can be fupported on the prefent iffue.

Thefe were the only points made in the caufe. Judgement being rendered for the defendant, the errors affigned were, that the court had miftaken the law on each of the points in queftion.

On the plea, *in nullo eft erratum*, it was now argued in this court.

Mr. *Reeve* and Mr. *Kirby*, for the plaintiffs in error.

It is an eftablifhed principle, that in mercantile companies, the contract of one partner, refpecting the partnerfhip, is binding on the whole, until notice of a diffolution be given.*—What is proper notice, and whether it has been given in this cafe, is a queftion.—The ordinary way of announcing fuch tranfactions is by advertifement in a public gazette. As each individual of the company acquires a joint credit with his copartners

1787.

Bradley
againft
Camp.

* Layfield's cafe.
1 Salkeld,
292.
2 Blackftone's Reports, 993.
Grace
againft
Smith.

copartners when that connection is formed, nothing can be more reasonable, than, that the
diffolution of that connection fhould be made
known wherever the company's dealings extend, before either can claim an exemption,
from the contracts of the other.—In the cafe
of *Fox* again/t *Hanbury*, *Cowper*, 449, it is adjudged by the court of King's Bench, that, " if
" partners diffolve their partnerfhip, they who
" deal with either, without notice of fuch dif-
" folution, have a right again/t both." That is
applying the rule more ftrictly than is neceffary
in the prefent cafe; for here was not the reafonable and ufual means of knowledge given.

Judge ELLSWORTH, mentioned the cafe of
Imlay, at Hartford, in which this point had been
adjudged. " The cafe was, that an action was
" brought again/t *William Imlay*, on a contract
" made by a partner of a company, (to which
" *Imlay* had belonged) after the diffolution.—
" It appeared that the diffolution had not been
" properly publifhed, and *Imlay* was holden to
" difcharge the debt."

The cafe of *Bloxham* and *Fourdrinier* again/t
Pell and *Brooke*, before Lord *Mansfield*, com-
pares very exactly with the prefent cafe.†———
" There was a partnerfhip for feven years be-
" tween *Brooke* and *Pell*; but at the end of one
" year agreed to be diffolved, but no exprefs
" diffolution was had.   The agreement recited,
" that *Brooke* being defirous to have the profits
" of the trade to himfelf, and *Pell* being defi-
" rous to relinquifh his right to the trade and
" profits, it was agreed, that *Brooke* fhould give
" *Pell* a bond for 2485*l*. which *Pell* had brought
" into trade, with intereft at *five per cent.* which
" was accordingly done.   And it was farther
" agreed, that *Brooke* fhould pay to *Pell* 200*l*.
" *per annum*, for fix years, if *Brooke* fo long li-
                                               " ved

† Cited in
2 Black-
ftone's Re-
ports, 999.

1786.

Bradley
againſt
Camp.

" ved, as in lieu of the profits of the trade ; and
" *Brooke* covenants, that *Pell* ſhould have free
" liberty to inſpect his books.—*Brooke* became
" a bankrupt before any thing was paid to *Pell*.
" And this action being brought for a debt in-
" curred by *Brooke,* in the courſe of trade, Lord
" *Mansfield* held that *Pell* was a ſecret partner."

In the caſe now under conſideration, there
was not a more expreſs diſſolution of the partnerſhip than in the one laſt mentioned ; for here
it was all verbal ; the terms being agreed upon,
two or three witneſſes only, were called to hear
the declaration of the parties concerned. There
it was committed to writing, and executed on
one ſide and on the other ; and though not publiſhed, it was as effectual. That was a much
harder caſe than the preſent ; for *Pell* not only
loſt all his ſtock in trade, and the profits covenanted to be paid him upon the diſſolution, but
was ſubject to pay the ſubſequent debts of his
partner. In the preſent caſe, *Camp* has ſaved
his ſtock in trade, and 200*l.* profit.

As to the ſecond point ;—the charges in this
caſe are of ſuch a kind, that if the diſſolution
had been publiſhed with the uſual formality, it
could not affect the preſent demand : For, unleſs there had been an expreſs ſtipulation that
this buſineſs ſhould be performed upon the ſole
credit of *Bingham,* or *Marvin* had been informed of the terms of the diſſolution, and that the
company dues were aſſigned to *Bingham,* and
had become his ſole property ; it muſt have been
preſumed a company concern, and for the benefit of all the partners, notwithſtanding the diſſolution. The diſſolution of a partnerſhip puts
an end to any future acqueſt of property from
the joint occupancy of the company's funds,
but it leaves the partners the ſame joint intereſt
in whatever they may have on hand, whether

L　　　　　　　it

1787.

Bradley
against
Camp.

it be in ſtock, debts due, or in any other form: And they ſtill continue to be partners, and as jointly liable as before, in every contract neceſſary to be made for the purpoſe of aſcertaining, collecting and dividing their property. And whatever compact there may be among the individuals, to controul this general authority, which each one ſtill retains of uſing the others credit on thoſe occaſions; ſtill, if that be not publiſhed, as well as the diſſolution, it can avail nothing, as it relates to ſtrangers.

The contract on which the preſent action is founded, is clearly of this kind; therefore, the right of recovery is not affected by a publication of the diſſolution.

As to the third point.——The demand in the preſent caſe originated from the proſecution of ſuits at law in the name of *Camp* and *Bingham*, for the recovery of debts contracted with them. Here was a joint intereſt held up to view; and *Camp*, by permitting *Bingham* thus to uſe his name, has empowered him to uſe his credit. If *Bingham* has abuſed the truſt repoſed in him, it is much more reaſonable that *Camp* ſhould ſuſtain the loſs, than a ſtranger.† Agreeable to this is the caſe of *Carvick* againſt *Vickery*, *Doug. Rep. append.* 31.

"This was an action by the indorſee of a bill "of exchange, which was in the following form:
    "Mr. *Abraham Vickery*,
"Two months after date, pleaſe to pay *to us* "or *our order*, the ſum of," &c.
        "*John Marydwell*,
        "*John Marydwell*, jun.
"It was endorſed thus—*John Marydwell*, jun.
"The *Marydwells* were father and ſon. The "endorſement was by the ſon. They were ad-"mitted not to be partners. The bill when "due, was preſented to the defendant, and ac-
        "cepted;

† 1. Salkeld, 289, Hern *against* Nickols. Holt 462, S. C. Durnf. 12. Fitzherbert *against* Mather.

" cepted; and at the ſame time he wrote upon
" it a direction to his banker to pay it. The
" plaintiff was non-ſuited, becauſe there was not
" an endorſement by both the parties to whoſe
" order the bill was made payable. A new trial
" was moved, on the ground, that the *Marydwells*
" by joining in the ſame bill, and holding them-
" ſelves out to the world as partners, ſhould
" therefore, for that purpoſe, be treated and
" dealt with as ſuch; and conſequently the en-
" dorſement of one was binding on the other.

" After argument, Lord *Mansfield* delivered
" the unanimous opinion of the court, that the
" *Marydwells*, by making the bill payable " *to*
" *our order*," had made themſelves partners as
" to this tranſaction."

In the preſent caſe there was as much appearance of a joint intereſt, as in the laſt mentioned, and more injuſtice might be done by not
treating it as ſuch.

The 4th point—whether, under the general
iſſue, the defendant may take exception, that
his partner is not deſcribed in the declaration
as having jointly contracted the debt with him.
—This point is fully ſettled in the books.

Contracts of this kind have ever been held to
be joint and ſeveral:—Being ſeveral, either of
the debtors may be proceeded againſt at the op-
tion of the creditor. And it cannot be eſſential
to the action, that the debt be deſcribed as contracted in company with another perſon. If it
be neceſſary thus to declare, it is merely for the
advantage of the defendant, that he may be better notified of the nature of the demand; therefore, being only matter of form, the exception
can never be taken but in abatement. If the
defendant neglects to take his exception at the
beginning of the ſuit, he is ſuppoſed to have
waved it. Theſe principles are fully eſtabliſh-

L 2   ed,

Bradley
against
Camp.

*5 Burrow,
2611, S.C.

ed, in the cafe of *Rice* vs. *Shute*, 2 *Blackſtone,*
697*—alfo, *Abot* vs. *Smith*, *ibidem* 947—*Sayer* vs.
Chaytor, *Lutwyche* 216—and *Gilbert* vs. *Bath,*
1 *Str.* 503.

The cafe of *Whitcomb* vs. *Whiting, Douglaſs*
629, furniſhes a precedent for this mode of declaring : " The declaration was in common
" form, on a promiſſory note executed by the
" defendant. The genezal iſſue was pleaded;
" and alfo *non aſſumpſit infra ſex annos;* replica-
" tion, *aſſumpſit infra ſex annos.* On trial, the
" plaintiff produced a joint and feveral note,
" executed by the defendant and three others."
This action proceeded, and no queſtion was
made as to the propriety of the procefs.

Mr. *Canfield* and Mr. *Strong*, for the defendant.——In this cafe there appears to have been
a copartnerſhip between the defendant and
Bingham. It, however, extended only to a ſingle ſtore of goods, and the authority that each
had to contract for the other, was reſtrained to
a fingle perfon. Under ſuch circumſtances, nothing more was neceſſary to deſtroy that authority, than to make the diſſolution of the company as extenſively known, as the exiſtence of it.
That was done in this cafe : It does not appear
that the partnerſhip had ever been heard of out
of the town of Saliſbury, except by Mrs. *Webb,*
at Wethersfield, with whom they traded; and it
is clear, that the creditor in this cafe had no
knowledge of it till the time of the contract.
Why, then, ought he to complain that he had
not notice of the diſſolution, when he did not
know of the company ? It is an idea not founded in reaſon, that the diſſolution of every company of merchants muſt be made known beyond
the limits of their ufual dealing. Notice would
never be neceſſary, but upon this ground,—that
the company, by reputation, having gained a credit,

dit, ſome act of equal notoriety, muſt take place
to put an end to it.   If this line be once paſſed, the partn⬤ can never be ſecure againſt each
other; for ſome one may always go where the
company hath not been known, and contract upon the credit of it.

It appears in this caſe, that at the ſame time
this debt was contracted, *Marvin* was tranſact-
ing the ſame kind of buſineſs for *Bingham*, on
his own credit.   It cannot therefore be ſuppoſed, that the credit of a company which he had
never before heard of, was the inducement to
undertake the proſecution of thoſe ſuits.   This
idea is corroborated by the length of time
which hath elapſed ſince the debt was contracted.
Had *Marvin* originally conſidered *Camp* to be
his debtor, he would undoubtedly have demanded payment long before this time : And had the
demand been within the life of *Bingham*, *Camp*
might have indemnified himſelf.   *Camp*, having
no knowledge of the contract, nor any notice of
the debt, it is unreaſonable, at this diſtance of
time, that he ſhould be holden.—The action of
book debt is founded on equitable principles;
and although *ſtricti juris*, there might be a right
of recovery; yet the court will duly weigh every,
circumſtance, that has equitably intervened in
favour of the defendant.

As to the laſt queſtion, it does not reſt ſimply
on this, whether there be a defect in point of
form; but the plaintiffs have declared, as upon
a contract with *Camp* only; the iſſue is, that the
defendant is not indebted in the manner and
form of the declaration.—The evidence exhibited on the trial is a contract with *Camp* and
Bingham.   This does not ſupport the iſſue.   It
is a debt of a different deſcription; and a recovery in the preſent caſe cannot be pleaded in
bar of another action upon the latter contract;

for

for the record will not ſhow it to be the ſame.—
The caſe of *Leglife* vs. *Champante*, 2. *Strange*,
820, is in point.———" There it appeared on
" evidence, that the plaintiff had a partner, who
" was not party to the action : And the Chief
" Juſtice (Lord *Raymond*) held, that if it was
" an *aſſumpſit*, it might be taken advantage of at
" the trial, for it would not be the ſame contract,
" but it ought to be pleaded in abatement in the
" caſe of a tort."

The *Chief Judge*, mentioned a caſe which had
been determined upon the authority of the caſe
now read from *Strange*; but ſaid the later authorities were the other way.

Judgement of the court of common pleas
reverſed.

By the whole Court.———A copartner-
ſhip in trade being formed, the partners become
liable to be jointly charged for all ſervices done,
or credits given at the requeſt of either of them,
relating to the buſineſs of the copartnerſhip ;
and ſo continue liable till public notice is given
of the copartnerſhip's being diſſolved. This is
neceſſary for the benefit of trade, and to prevent
impoſition ; and ſo far as the right each partner
derives from the formation of the partnerſhip,
to contract for the company, relates to creditors, that right is not vacated, until public notice
of a diſſolution is given.—*Cowper*, 449, *Fox* vs.
Hanbury.——In the preſent caſe, this notice was
not given, nor had the creditor any knowledge
of the fact, He might well, therefore, charge
the partners in company ; more eſpecially, as
the ſervices he rendered were *prima facie* for
their joint benefit, being the proſecution of ſuits
in their joint names, and which aroſe out of the
company tranſactions.

There can be no doubt but a right of action
ſurvived againſt the ſurviving partner ; eſpecially

ly if it be confidered, that all company contracts are in their nature joint and feveral : And as to the manner of bringing this fuit, it might have been well for the purpofes of certainty, and benefit of the defendant, in preparing his defence, to have declared, that the debt was contracted by the defendant in company with *Bingham* : But a failure thus to declare, was only pleadable in abatement, and could be of no avail under the general iffue, on which the caufe was tried.* For it doth not falfify a charge of debt againft one, to fhow that another is alfo indebted, and might have been joined in the fuit : Nor doth the law require the fame circumftantiality and precifion in declaring upon fpecialities, or other writings of which there is a profit, as on a fpecial affumpfit, where the defendant has no means of identifying the contract but from the declaration ; and a fmall variation between the allegations and the proofs may be fatal.

Therefore, the judgement of the court of common pleas was reverfed.

1787.

Bradley
againft
Camp.

* 2 Blackftone's *Reports* 697,
Rice
vs
Shute.
5 Burrow,
2611. S. C.
2 Blackftone, 947,
Abot
vs
Smith.

The State *againft* William Green.

THIS was an indictment for adultery.—— After verdict, Mr. *Reeve* and Mr. *Tracy*, counfel for the prifoner, moved in arreft. They fhowed for caufe,—That the teftimony produced againft the prifoner, on trial, was, that fome perfons fufpecting faid *Green* to be with *Tryphena*, wife of *Samuel Roffetar*, at 9 o'clock in the evening of the 10th day of May 1786, and that they fet out to go to the houfe of *Roffetar*, and were told that faid *Tryphena* had faid fhe fhould

The jury are to judge of the weight of evidence, taking into confideration, every circumftance of the cafe ; therefore, teftimony which is thought by them fufficient to convict on an indictment for

adultery, is conclufive after verdict ; even if the court fhould be of a different opinion

lodge at a neighbour's houfe that night: They, however, went to the houfe, and found the doors faftened. They then went to the neighbour's houfe mentioned, and found fhe was not there. —They returned again to *Roffetar's* houfe, and having heard fome perfon nailing a window, they ▮▮▮▮ in and found *Green* in bed with faid *Tryp▮▮n▮*, a little after 10 o'clock in the evening; and fhe was feen to turn from *Green* while in bed undreffed: Which f▮ct was not contefted by the counfel affigned f▮ ▮ the prifoner; but the whole matter in difpute was, whether that faat was fufficient to convict upon the ftatute againft adultery:—And that the verdict was found againft law.

For the prifoner they urged, that this was not proof of the crime of adultery; though it was undoubted proof of a different crime of a lower nature, for which the legiflature have exprefsly provided a punifhment, by ftatute; which is— " That if any man be found in bed with another " man's wife, the man and woman fo offending, " being thereof convicted, fhall be feverely " whipt, not exceeding thirty ftripes."—This ftatute was exprefsly provided for cafes like the prefent, where clear proof cannot be had of the act of adultery; for the law will not punifh men with the feverity affixed to the crime of adultery, upon mere prefumption.

The motion over ruled.

By the whole Court.——The jury are by law the proper judges of the weight of evidence, on the whole circumftances of the cafe: And although the prifoner, by the fame teftimony, might have been proceeded againft and convicted on another ftatute, for a lower offence; yet it cannot from thence be inferred, that the evidence was not fufficient to convict him of adultery.

Note.

Note.—In this cafe motion was made for the admiffion of a witnefs, to prove that the prifoner, at a time previous to the crime alledged, hired this witnefs to go to the houfe, and fee whether the woman's hufband was at home.

Objected by the prifoner's counfel, becaufe it was no part of the facts alledged in the indictment.

The witnefs was admitted: For,

By the whole Court.——Though it is no part of the direct charge in the indictment, it is a circumftance which leads to the crime.

Anonimous.

THE Court faid it was an eftablifhed rule, when judgement is arrefted after verdict for the infufficiency of the declaration, not to tax coft on either fide.

Mills *againft* Bishop.

THIS cafe was determined on pleas in abatement the laft term, and the plaintiff allowed to amend on paying coft: Final judgement being now rendered for the plaintiff, he offered his whole coft to be taxed; but it was ruled by *the whole court*, that the plaintiff fhould recover no coft antecedent to the abatement, excepting writ, duty, and officers fees.

On firft judgment in f vor of a plaintiff, after a bate-ment and a-mendment, the plaintiff fhall recover to coft, antecedent to the amendment, excepting writ, duty and officers fees.

Wooster *againft* Simons.

THIS cafe was tried at the court of common pleas, on the general iffue, and a verdict for the plaintiff.——The defendant moved in

The defendant cannot demur to the declaration, after having pleaded to iffue.

M

1786.

Wooster
against
Simons.

arreft, becaufe of the infufficiency of the declaration; which was over-ruled.—The defendant then appealed; and before this court, moved for leave to demur to the declaration; which was denied *by the court*: Becaufe, by ftatute, the defendant having pleaded to iffue, and judgement thereon been rendered, fhall not demur.

———

GRANT *against* JACKSON.

Declaration, "that the defendant received of the plaintiff 29*l*. 6*s*. 8*d*. in orders on the one shilling tax, which he promifed to return or account for;" adjudged infufficient for uncertainty.

ASSUMPSIT.——The declaration is,—
"That on the 23d day of Sept. 1784, the "defendant received of the plaintiff 29*l*. 6*s*. 8*d*. "in orders on the one fhilling tax; which orders "the defendant then and there promifed to re-"turn to the plaintiff by the firft day of July "then next, or to account with the plaintiff for "faid orders in fome other way, by faid time; "as appears by a writing under the defendant's "hand, of the date above, ready in court to be "produced."

To this declaration the defendant demurred generally.

Mr. *Strong*, for the defendant, took two exceptions:—

1. The declaration is fo vague and uncertain, that no legal judgement can be founded thereon. It does not point out the kind of orders with that certainly that the value can be afcertained.

2. The action is mifconceived, for by the plaintiff's own fhewing the defendant was to account; the action therefore ought to have been *account* and not *affumpfit*.

Mr. *Tracy* for the plaintiff.——The declaration counts truly on the writing, and ftates the whole

whole of it; it could not with propriety go any further.—The defendant ſuffers no diſadvantage; for he is ſufficiently notified of the nature and kind of the demand.—If there be any uncertainty reſpecting the damage to be aſſeſſed, it may be aided by evidence.

As to the ſecond exception, aſſumpſit will lie in all caſes where there is an expreſs undertaking to account.—1. *Salkeld*, 9. *Wilkin* vs. *Wilkin.*—1. *Bacon's Abr. tit. aſſumpſit.* (A.)

By the whole Court.——The declaration is inſufficient; it gives no rule of damages. The orders which the defendant is challenged to account for being no otherwiſe deſcribed than as drawn on the one ſhilling tax; and as it doth not appear by whom or by what authority they were drawn, or on which of the one ſhilling taxes, as divers have been granted and were of different values, there is no rule given to the court by which to aſcertain their value, or aſſeſs damages for not re-delivering or otherwiſe accounting for them.

The Eccleſiaſtical Society *of* South-Farms *in* Litchfield, *againſt* George Beckwith.

ACTION for breach of covenant.—The declaration was, that the plaintiffs having called the defendant, in the cuſtomary way of calling candidates for the miniſtry, to ſettle with them as a goſpel miniſter; and he having covenanted and agreed to the ſame; for the better underſtanding and mutual advantage of the parties, at Litchfield, on the 22d day of October 1772, the plaintiffs and defendant covenanted

M 2   and

and agreed, among other things, as follows:
viz.. " The *church* and *society (meaning the church*
" *formed in said society, and the inhabitants of*
" *said society)* engage to support Mr. *Beckwith*
" during his natural life, and to give him 135l.
" on the day of his installation; and if not paid
" at that time, to pay him the interest thereof
" till paid. Also to pay him 65l. more, with-
" in two years from said time, and if not then
" paid, to pay him the interest thereof till
" paid. All this, the said *church* and *society*
" agree to pay Mr. *Beckwith* as a settlement.
" And the said Mr. *Beckwith*, on his part doth
" hereby agree to accept the above offer, and en-
" gage to become the minister and pastor of said
" *church* upon their present establishment; and
" to serve said *church* and *society* in the gospel
" ministry, as God shall give him ability, during
" his natural life; and not to vary or go off
" from said establishment, without a majority
" of said *church* and *society* collectively, except
" he forfeit (if it be immediately) his whole set-
" tlement; if after but one year from the time
" of his settlement, then 190l. thereof; if after
" two years, then 180l.—and so on in the same
" proportion, according to the number of years
" he continues to be their pastor, till twenty
" years are expired, if God please to spare his
" life, and continue said near relation till after
" that time, when after that there shall be no
" forfeiture of settlement." Which covenant
was well executed under the hands and seals of
a committee lawfully authorifed by said *church*
and *society*, and by the defendant, dated the 22d
day of October 1772; as appears by said covenant ready in court to be shown.

And the plaintiffs say, the establishment
which the defendant in said covenant agrees and
promises not to vary or go off from, without the
majority

majority of ſaid *church* and *ſociety*, under the penalty of forfeiting, as is mentioned in ſaid covenant, was underſtood and meant by the parties
at ſaid time, to be the eſtabliſhment or mode
of church diſcipline, then practiſed by ſaid
church and *ſociety*; which was, as the defendant
very well knew, the ſame eſtabliſhment adopted
in general by preſbyterians, and congregational
churches in the ſtate of Connecticut, commonly
called *Saybrook-Platform eſtabliſhment*, or form
of church diſcipline. And that ſaid 135l. and
ſaid 65l. promiſed to the defendant in ſaid covenant, was meant lawful money, and in lawful
money was actually paid to the defendant by the
plaintiffs, agreeably to the covenant aforeſaid.
Yet, the defendant, not ignorant of the premiſes, and diſregarding his covenant and agreement, on the 5th day of January 1773, knowing he was liable to cenſure for ſome of his conduct, and being called upon by the aſſociation
for Litchfield county, to anſwer for his ſaid
conduct. To obey which requeſt of the aſſociation, the defendant was obliged by the known
conſtitution, and eſtabliſhment of ſaid *church*,
and all the churches adopting *Saybrook-Platform*, for a mode of diſcipline. And for the
purpoſe of avoiding a ſcrutiny of his conduct, by
ſaid aſſociation, privately convened the members of ſaid *church*, and without the knowledge,
or conſent of the inhabitants of ſaid *ſociety*, the
defendant and majority of ſaid *church*, paſſed a
number of votes, or propoſitions, reſpecting the
mode of church diſcipline, for their future practice; which they attempted to ſupport and countenance by many ſcripture proofs, totally ſub-
verſive, and directly contrary to the plan of
church diſcipline, formerly adopted by ſaid
church; and directly contrary to the plan or
mode of church-government, which was meant
and

and intended by the parties in ſaid covenant, not to be varied or altered by the defendant, without his incurring the forfeitures mentioned in ſaid covenant. Particularly, the plaintiffs ſay, the majority of ſaid *church*, under the influence and inſtigation of the defendant, and to avoid a ſcrutiny of his conduct as aforeſaid— voted in, agreed to, and have ever ſince acted upon, until the defendants diſmiffion from ſaid *ſociety*, among many propoſitions, the following, viz.

" That all powers, authorities, capacities, and " privileges, which in the holy ſcriptures are " ſaid to belong, or appertain to the church of " Chriſt, do belong to every particular church ; " and that every ſuch particular church is reſ- " ponſible to Jeſus Chriſt for the exerciſe of " ſuch powers, abilities and privileges, to them " by him annexed ; and conſequently by divine " conſtitution are inherent and eſſential, and ſo " can never be transfered or aſſigned over to " others. And therefore it is the intereſt and " eſſential right of every particular church, to " chooſe its own paſtor, and all means requi- " ſite and neceſſary to render ſuch a choice ef- " fectual. Alſo to exerciſe diſcipline over its " own members, according to the will of Chriſt ; " and that no other *church, confociation of church-* " *es, or ecclefiaftical council* whatever, has, or can " have, any right authoritatively to intermeddle " with matters of this kind. And that therefore, " the claims made by the *affociation of Litchfield* " *county*, to examine all licenſed candidates for " the miniſtry before they may give an anſwer " to an invitation, or accept an invitation to the " paſtoral office in ſaid county ; alſo the late " claim of the confociation of ſaid county, to " exerciſe an excluſive right of ordaining to the " paſtoral office ; and authoritatively and deci-
" ſively

" fively determine matters ecclefiaftical within
" faid county, is, in the opinion of this *church*,
" an infringement upon chriftian liberty, and
" inconfiftent with the fimplicity of the gof-
" pel, and the rights of churches; and that
" by the laws of Jefus Chrift, this *church* is
" indifpenfibly obliged not to fubmit to a-
" ny authority, claimed as aforefaid.   And
" that it is the opinion of the *church*, upon
" mature deliberation, that the articles of
" agreement, *(as they are called)* confidered as a
" fyftem, faid to be entered into by the church-
" es in Litchfield county, ought never to be, or
" to have been confidered as a rule to be obferv-
" ed by this *church*."   As by faid vote or pro-
pofition ready in court to be produced, may appear; dated January the 5th day, A. D. 1773.

Which conduct of the defendant, in varying,
going off from, and entirely altering the eftablifhment of faid *church*, as to difcipline, and without the knowledge or confent of faid *fociety*, was
a direct violation of his covenant with the plaintiffs, as mentioned above.   And by which conduct, the plaintiffs fay, he has forfeited his fettlement, according to the tenor of faid covenant; and by which means they are entitled by
law to recover of the defendant, as they fay,
500l. lawful money.

To this declaration, Mr. *Adams* and Mr.
Canfield, for the defendant, demurred generally; under which they took the following exceptions:

1. The declaration does not fet forth with
fufficient certainty, what the conftitution of the
church was, fo as to admit of proof or difproof;
it is only ftated by way of innuendo.

2. That the whole matter is merely fpiritual.
It is only whether the defendant has taught the
beft fcripture doctrine; which is a matter the
court can never take cognizance of.

3. The

3. The defendant only acted as moderator of the church meeting; and the votes alledged as a breach of his covenant, were the act of the church, and not his act, or imputable to him as a sole transaction; which only could be a breach on his part; for no act of the church can be imputed to the defendant, either as a breach, or fulfilment of the covenant.

4. There is nothing stated in the declaration, which can operate as a rule of certainty, whereby damages may be given; for it is no where averred at what time the defendant was ordained or installed, or how long he continued in the performance of his covenants.

Mr. *Reeve* and Mr. *Tracy*, for the plaintiffs.

In answer to the first exception, the declaration expressly avers, that the constitution of church-discipline, meant and understood by the contracting parties, and which the defendant covenanted not to deviate from, was the *Saybrook-Platform.* That is a system of church-government, which has become a part of the laws of the land, and therefore can need no further definition.

2. This cannot be considered as an ecclesiastical matter; the contract and covenant is wholly civil, and it is as easy to determine, whether the defendant has acted in conformity to the principles of the church-constitution, as to determine any other fact.

3. The votes stated by the plaintiffs, amount to a direct declaration of independance. It is averred that the defendant procured the *church*, to pass those votes which contain a system totally repugnant to the *Saybrook-Platform.* The activity of the defendant to procure those votes, is a single act alledged against him capable of being traversed. And it is further averred that he immediately went on, and has ever since practised on those principles.

4. The

1786.

South-
Farms
againft
Beckwich.

4. The breach of the covenant muft have reference to the making of it. The inftant the
covenant was compleated, they became bound
to pay him fo much money, he became their minifter, and was obliged to practice by the rules
and principles pointed out by the contracting
parties. Any deviation from thofe rules, after
that, was a breach of the covenant.

BY THE WHOLE COURT—The declaration is
infufficient.—Becaufe, 1ft, The rule of damages is uncertain.—The claim is, that the defendant fhould repay, as a forfeiture, a part of his
fettlement, proportioned to the time from his
inftallation, to a certain fubfequent period, when
he is fuppofed to have broken his covenant;
but when his inftallation took place, doth not
appear from the declaration.

2. It doth not appear that the covenant hath
been broken.—The covenant was, on the part
of the defendant, that he fhould be the minifter
of faid *church*, as then eftablifhed, (which is faid
to have been upon the *Saybrook-Platform)* and
" not vary or go off from faid eftablifhment,
without a major part of the *church* and *fociety*."
They might, if they faw fit, releafe him or al-
ter their eftablifhment; but otherwife he was
bound by this covenant to continue their minifter, and to conform to the rules and difcipline of
faid *church*, as then practiced and eftablifhed,
under certain penalties. This was the extent
of his covenant; and of this, it doth not appear
that he has, in any point failed. It was no
breach, on his part, that the *church*, for whofe
conduct he had not ftipulated, and whofe proceedings he had not power to direct or ne-
gate, paffed certain votes, and declared certain
claims of the *confociated churches in Litchfield
county*, unfcriptural. How far thofe claims were
warranted by the *Saybrook-Platform*, or how

N   far

far the *church*, by declaring againſt them, has affected its conſtitution, is not material, ſince it doth not appear that the defendant has ever refuſed to ſubmit to, or adminiſter diſcipline in ſaid *church*, or to perform the other duties of a paſtor thereof, according to the rules eſtabliſhed and practiced therein, at the time of his ſettlement. The averment, that ever ſince the aforeſaid declaration, he has practiced agreeably thereto, is too general. It is not traverſable. Nor can it appear to the court, unleſs the facts, or ſome of them, are ſpecially ſet forth, that the conduct of the defendant, has amounted to a breach of his covenant.

Church *againſt* Thomson.

Working
unfealed
leather into
faddles and
harnefs, is
held, by
three judges
againft two,
not to be
within the
ftatute, re-
gulating
tanners.

INFORMATION *qui tam*, on the ſtatute for working unſealed leather.——By the ſtatute, it is enacted, " That no perſon or perſons whatſoever ſhall cauſe or ſuffer any leather by him or them tanned, to be wrought " up by any ſhoemaker, employed either by " himſelf, or by any other perſon or perſons " for him ; nor ſhall he work up the ſame himſelf, before ſuch leather be viewed and ſealed, " as aforeſaid, on penalty of forfeiting the ſum " of *five pounds* for every hide or ſkin ſo as " aforeſaid by him or them wrought, cauſed " or ſuffered to be wrought up, before ſealing " as aforeſaid."

The defendant was a tanner, and had worked unſealed leather into ſaddles and harneſs : It was not clearly proved that he had worked any into ſhoes, though the circumſtances rendered it very probable.

The

The jury found a verdict for the plaintiff, on which the Court delivered the following opinions:— -

LAW, *Chief Juſtice*, SHERMAN and ELLSWORTH,—Suppoſed that clauſe of the ſtatute to have reference to ſhoes and boots only; and that it could not be extended beyond the letter, ſo as to include ſaddles and harneſs; it being a penal ſtatute, ought to be conſtrued ſtrictly, otherwiſe it might operate as a ſnare to mankind.

DYER and PITKIN,—ſaid they conſidered the law to be every where pointedly againſt manufacturing or vending bad leather: That the great object of the ſtatute is to prevent that public injury. The working of bad leather into ſaddles and other wares, is as expreſsly within the miſchief the law intended to prevent, as the working of it into ſhoes; therefore within the ſpirit and meaning. *Nam qui hæret in litera, hæret in cortice.*

CLAP

CLAP *againſt* LOCKWOOD *and Others.*

1786.

When number-
bers are
joined in a
ſuit ; depo-
ſitions can-
not be im-
proved a-
gainſt ſuch
of them as
are not no-
tified of the
taking ; but
each perſon
muſt have
notice ; if
within the
diſtance,
the ſtatute
preſcribes.

THIS was an action of trover againſt ſeveral defendants.—Mr. *Davenport,* for the
plaintiff, offered to read a depoſition taken out
of court; but it appeared that one of the defendants was neither notified or preſent at the
taking thereof, although he lived within four
miles of the place of caption. And,

BY THE COURT,—It was rejected, as it reſpected the defendant not notified; becauſe
the defendants have a right to plead ſeverally;
and they may have different defences; and the
queſtions put by thoſe who were preſent may
be inapplicable to the defence of the one not
preſent, and he might thereby be defeated of
the benefit of croſs-examination.

STEPHEN GOLD.—*Appeal from Probate.*

A Judge of
Probate
ought not to
reject an in-
ven ory,
that contains
property ;
the title to
which s diſ-
puted : for
his deciſion
cannot aff. &
the ight of
trying the ti-
tle to proper-
ty, at com-
mon law.

MR. *Benedict* and Mr. *Whittleſey,* for the
appellant, aſſigned the following reaſons
for their appeal :—That the appellant is one of
the heirs of *Hezekiah Burr,* deceaſed ; and that
ſaid *Burr,* in his life-time, was well ſeized and
poſſeſſed, in his own right in *fee ſimple,* of a
certain tract of land, lying in Reading, in the
county of Fairfield, containing about one hundred and ſixty acres, bounded, &c. and continued thereof ſo ſeized until his death, which
happened, &c. Upon the deceaſe of ſaid *Burr,*
the ſaid eſtate deſcended to the appellant,
Sarah Jackſon and others, heirs of the ſaid *deceaſed,* and they became thereof ſeized in fee.
At a court of probate, held at *Danbury,* &c.
the

the appellant was duly appointed adminiftrator on the eftate of faid *Burr*, he having died inteftate. And at a court of probate, held at faid Danbury, on the 13th day of January, A. D. 1786, an *inventory*, made in due form of law, was by the appellant exhibited to faid court; and the appellant, on fuch exhibition, did pray faid court to admit proper proof of the fame, and on fuch proof, to approve and record faid *inventory*; and the faid court did refufe to admit proof of faid *inventory*, and did difapprove thereof.

Mr. *Ingerfol* and Mr. *Rowland* replied,— That faid appeal ought to be difmiffed; becaufe all faid lands mentioned and contained in faid inventory, were by the inteftate, during his life, granted and conveyed to the *appellees*, by deed of *bargain and fale*, figned, fealed, delivered, and duly acknowledged before proper authority, dated the 7th day of *February*, A. D. 1780, and during the life of the inteftate was recorded according to law; by force whereof faid appellees became feized in fee of all faid land; and being fo feized, ftill continue to be fo feized thereof: And that, at the time of the death of faid *Hezekiah Burr*, he was not feized or poffeffed in fee of faid land, and had not any intereft therein; wherefore, the fame could not be inventoried as his eftate: And that the appellees were, by the Judge of Probate, duly notified to appear, and fhew reafon why faid inventory fhould not be accepted: And faid appellees appeared before faid Judge, and claimed faid land, at the fame time faid inventory was produced and offered for acceptance; and on exhibiting faid deed, and reading the fame to faid Judge of Probate, he refufed to approve of faid inventory, and did difapprove thereof.

The

The appellant rejoined, that the inteſtate, at the time of executing ſaid deed, was of unſound mind, and incapable of making any contract; and therefore ſaid deed is void in law: And the appellant, at the time of exhibiting ſaid inventory, offered to prove to ſaid court, that the inteſtate, at the time of executing and delivering ſaid deed, was of unſound mind and memory, and for want of underſtanding, incapable of making any contract or bargain; and the ſaid Judge refuſed to admit any ſuch proof.

To this, there was a demurrer, and joinder in demurrer.

The exception was, that the court of probate ought not to accept or approve of an inventory, when it appears upon record, that the real eſtate ſo inventoried is claimed, and the title veſted in ſome other perſon. The adminiſtrator had fully diſcharged his duty, when he exhibited his inventory to the court of probate; and whether accepted or refuſed, the adminiſtrator cannot afterwards be liable.

Mr. *Benedict* and Mr. *Whittleſey*, on the other ſide.——The adminiſtrator being under oath to a faithful diſcharge of his duty, is ſuppoſed to know what is the proper eſtate of the deceaſed to be inventoried. The doings of the court of probate cannot affect the title; therefore, no one is injured by having eſtate inventoried which he may claim. The adminiſtrator ought to be careful to inventory the whole eſtate of the inteſtate, for his own ſecurity againſt the creditors, and to ſave his bond, as well as to prevent the heirs (if any) from recovering judgement in their own right, of the eſtate, and thereby exclude it from the hands of the adminiſtrator.

The decree of the court of probate reverſed. And,

BY THE WHOLE COURT.——It was the
duty

duty of the adminiftrator to exhibit an inventory of all the eftate, real and perfonal, that he had reafon to fuppofe belonged to the inteftate: And if any part of faid eftate is claimed by any other perfon, the parties have right to try the title at common law, and cannot be concluded by the judgement of a court of probate. In cafe the eftate belonged to the inteftate, the adminiftrator could not profecute his claim, or apply the property for the payment of debts (if neceffary) until it was inventoried. To inventory the eftate here objected to, might be neceffary for the adminiftrator, to comply with his duty and truft, and could be prejudicial to no one elfe; the inventory he offered, ought therefore to have been received, and the court of probate erred in rejecting it.

COOLEY *againft* SANFORD.

ACTION on mutual promifes *(to wit)* That if the plaintiff acquired a good title to certain lands, which he had attached as the property of one *Guyer*, and fhould make a good conveyance of faid lands in fee fimple to the defendant, then the defendant engaged to become obligated to the plaintiff in the fum of 209*l.* payable in a reafonable time; which agreement was in writing, with a penal claufe.

The cafe was, that the plaintiff ferved his writ of attachment upon the land mentioned, on the 15th day of May, 1783, in the afternoon; and on the 22d, in the forenoon, a copy was left with the town-clerk, which was not
attefted

atteſted to be a true copy ; and there were ſeveral variations between *that* and the one left
in ſervice, and alſo between the return on *that*
and on the original writ: The boundary on
one ſide was deſcribed in a different manner.

After the ſervice of this attachment on the
lands, and before the copy was left with the
town-clerk, the defendant, *Sanford*, knowing
thereof, purchaſed the land of *Guyer*, the
debtor, and received a deed of bargain and
ſale, dated the 21ſt day of May, 1783, and
recorded the ſame day.

On the 11th day of Auguſt, 1783; the agreement was made between the plaintiff and defendant.   The plaintiff afterwards recovered
judgement againſt *Guyer*, had execution, and
levied on the land in legal form.   The plaintiff then tendered to the defendant an ample
deed of the land, and demanded the obligation
for 209*l.* but the defendant refuſed.

This action being brought, and iſſue joined
to the court, the only queſtion was, whether
Cooley, under all the circumſtances, had acquired a good title to the land, ſo as to be able
to convey, agreeably to the tenor of the agreement.

Mr. *Benedict* and Mr. *Ingerſol,* for the defendant:—There ought to have been the ſame
kind of atteſtation to the copy left with the
town-clerk, as to the copy left with the party
in ſervice ; and if not the ſame literal exactneſs
throughout, yet there ought to be the moſt cri-
tical exactneſs in the deſcription of the lands
taken, otherwiſe they are not identified, and
the copy ſo left can anſwer no purpoſe but to
miſlead : In the preſent caſe, there being no
atteſted copy left with the town-clerk; and the
pretended copy ſo left, being eſſentially vari-
ant from the original, and from the one left in
ſervice

fervice with the party, it could create no lien on tne land; therefore, the fubfequent pur-chafe by Sanford has given him an ample title.

Mr. Chauncey and Mr. Sillinian, for the plain-tiff.—The law requires no more than a certi-ficate, or defcription of the eftate taken, to be left with the town-clerk. The words of the ftatute are, " When any real eftate is taken, " the officer ferving the writ fhall leave a true " and attefted copy thereof, and a defcription " of the eftate taken, at the town-clerk's office, " in the town where the eftate lies; and until " the fervice is completed, the eftate fo at- " tached fhall not be held by fuch attachment, " againft any other creditor or bona-fide pur- " chafer." The object of the law can be no more than to give notice to the world of the lien that is on the land: This purpofe was ful-ly anfwered in the prefent cafe, by the copy that was left; and the land was fo far defcribed, that no miftake could have happened in regard to it; the officer, therefore, has fubftantially performed his fervice.

The deed from Guyer to Sanford, was ob-tained under fuch circumftances, that the tranf-action contains in it a fraud: Sanford was ac-quainted with the circumftances; he undoubt-edly defigned to defeat Cooley of his hold upon the land; he therefore took it in his own wrong, which cannot legally operate to his be-nefit.

Judgement was rendered for the plaintiff.

The

The State *against* Samuel Lockwood, 3d.

The superior court may take cognizance of the crime of perjury and forgery.

INFORMATION for *perjury*.—Mr. *Davenport*, of counsel for the prisoner, objected to the jurisdiction: He urged, that the court of common pleas is the only court which by law can take cognizance of the crime of *perjury*: That by high crimes and misdemeanors, mentioned in the statute, is intended only such high offences as have no express punishment by law annexed; and as the statute has ascertained the punishment for perjury, which does not extend to life, limb, or banishment, it cannot be cognizable by the superior court.

Judge Ellsworth observed, That in a case of forgery at Windham, the same exception was taken, and over-ruled by the court: And,

The Court held, that they might take cognizance of the crime of perjury.

Dauchy *against* Smith *and* Olmsted.

A demurrer to a declaration, containing a recital of the obligation on which the suit is founded, is ill, for any allegation of variance; the advantage should be taken by abatement on oyer, or demurrer to evidence.

THIS was an action of debt on bond; the declaration in common form.

Mr. *Ingersol* prayed oyer of the bond, which he recited at large in his plea, and concluded by demurring to the declaration.

The bond appeared to have been taken to the plaintiff, in the capacity of *constable* of the town of Ridgefield. It was conditioned that *Smith*, one of the obligors, should appear before the court of common pleas, at Fairfield, on the third Tuesday of April, 1784, answer to an action, in favour of *James Sturges*, against him

him, plead in cuftody of the court, and not depart without licence.

Mr. *Inge* took two exceptions under the demurrer:—

1. That the bond being taken by an officer in his official capacity, the condition ought to have been expreſſed in the declaration; for otherwise it does not appear but that it was taken for eafe and favour, which would be illegal. Although it does not appear upon the face of the declaration that the bond was taken to an officer, yet, by inferting it in the plea, the whole becomes parcel of the record; and the advantage may in this manner be as well taken under a demurrer as by pleading a variance.

2. The condition of the bond is unwarrantable: For it is, that *Smith* fhall appear and plead in cuftody: That he fhall fuffer imprifonment at all events; which defeats the very defign of bail.

By THE WHOLE COURT.——For ought that appears from the declaration, a good and fufficient bond is declared upon, and well defcribed; and if the defendants would avail themfelves of any variance between the bond declared upon and that fhown upon oyer, they fhould have taken advantage of it by plea in abatement, or demurrer to the evidence; the declaration, therefore, adjudged fufficient.

Note,—*This adjudication is oppoſed to the Engliſh practice—vide* 2. Wilſon's Reports, 339, Turner *vs.* Vaughan.

NORTHROP

1786.

If a Justice of Peace does not certify in a binding over for a secret assault, that the complainant showed his wounds, and made oath to the facts, it is matter of abatement, and not demurrable.

And if two persons assault another, no witness being present, both may be joined in the complaint for a private assault.

NORTHROP *against* BRUSH *and* ISAACS.

THIS was an action on the statute against secret assaults, wherein it is enacted,—
" That if any person shall break the peace, by
" secretly assaulting, beating, maiming, wound-
" ing, or hurting another, the person so af-
" saulted and injured, making application and
" complaining to the next assistant or justice of
" the peace, showing him what hurt or wounds
" he has received thereby; such assistant or jus-
" tice shall forthwith grant out a writ to the she-
" riff of the county, or his deputy, or constable
" of the town where such assault shall be made,
" commanding them, or either of them, to
" arrest and bring before him such person so
" assaulting, to answer such complaint; who,
" upon oath being made against him of such
" assault, and of the wounds or bruises there-
" by received by the person so assaulted and
" beaten, shall be bound in a sufficient bond,
" &c."

The complaint was, that the defendant, *Brush*, invited *Northrop* to the coffee-house, in New-Haven, into a private room, under the pretence of business, and did there assault the plaintiff with loaded pistols, &c. That the other defendant, *Isaacs*, came into the room, and did combine with *Brush*; and that they did further assault and beat the plaintiff, no other person being present.

The justice who bound over the defendants did not certify that the plaintiff was admitted to his oath, or had discovered his wounds.

And under a general demurrer two exceptions were taken:

1. That it did not appear from the process that the plaintiff ever charged the defendants

under

under oath, with the facts complained of, or that he shewed his wounds to the justice, which the statute makes necessary to support this kind of action.

2. That the assault complained of was not in its nature such as is intended by the statute; it was committed in a public place, and by a plurality of persons; the plaintiff, therefore, may have his remedy at common law: But,

BY THE WHOLE COURT,—The complaint is sufficient. As to the first exception, that the complainant did not show his wounds, and make oath before the justice; such oath and exhibition were proper evidence for the justice to proceed upon, and the presumption is, they were had, unless there was an admission of the facts to render them unnecessary: It was not necessary for the justice to set forth the evidence he proceeded upon; or if it was, his omission to do it should have been pleaded in abatement. The demurrer goes not to the certainty or regularity of the process, but to the sufficiency of the complaint.

As to the second exception, that it was not a secret assault, because committed by two persons: Two persons may commit an assault jointly; and if it is out of the presence or view of others, it is a secret assault; and although the person assaulted *may* proceed against one of them in a common action of trespass, and take the other for a witness, yet he is not obliged to pursue that method: One of them alone may be insufficient to repair the damages; and it may also be unsafe for him to rest on the testimony of a person whose malignity had induced him to join in a secret attack upon his person; and it is for the public peace and safety, that both the assailants should be complained of, that they may be punished criminaliter.

naliter. This aſſault, though made by two perſons, is within the ſtatute againſt ſecret aſſault.

Note.—*This judgement was afterwards affirmed in the ſupreme court of errors.*

WOOSTER *againſt* PARSONS.

In an action for falſe impriſonment the defendant juſtifies under the authority of an inferior court. Replication, that the court had no jurisdiction, adjudged inſufficient; becauſe the want of juriſdiction does not appear upon the face of the proceſs, and it is too late to ſhew it by matter dehors the record.

THIS was an action of trespaſs for falſe impriſonment.—The defendant pleaded that he inſtituted a ſuit againſt the plaintiff, on a promiſſory note, before the city court, in the city of Middletown, and obtained judgement thereon, by default: That execution was duly granted upon ſaid judgement, by virtue of which the plaintiff was taken and impriſoned; which is the ſame and only impriſonment complained of.

Replication.—That ſaid note was given, executed and delivered without the city of Middletown: That the cauſe of action, which was the foundation of ſaid judgement, did not ariſe within the limits of ſaid city; therefore, ſaid court had not juriſdiction of ſaid cauſe, and ought not to have rendered judgement and iſſued execution thereon.

On demurrer to this replication, judgement was rendered for the defendant, by *the whole court* :—And by

DYER, SHERMAN and PITKIN, *Judges*.— The plaintiff's reply is inſufficient; becauſe it is not therein alledged, that the defendant knew that the cauſe of action aroſe out of the juriſdiction of the *city court:* For if the plaintiff, in the action before the *city court*, had averred in his

his declaration, that the cauſe of action aroſe within the juriſdiction of the court, when he knew it did not; it would, as to him, have been a proceſs unduly obtained, and action of falſe impriſonment would lie againſt him, though not againſt the officer *(Lilly's Abrid.* 695.) If it had appeared on the face of the proceſs that the cauſe of action did ariſe out of the juriſdiction of the city court, all the proceedings would have been *coram non judice,* and void, and could have been no juſtification or ex-cuſe for any thing done under them; nor would any neglect to plead it, or any conceſſion of the parties make it good. 2. *Modern Reports,* 29.

In the preſent caſe it was not alledged, that the cauſe of action did ariſe within the juriſdiction of the city court, and for that and other reaſons, the judgement has been re-verſed; * but the preſent defendant might have been ignorant, or miſtaken as to the place where the cauſe of action did ariſe; and in that caſe he would not be liable to this action. 2. *Wilſon's Reports, from* 302 *to* 308.

LAW, *Chief Juſtice,* and ELLSWORTH, *Judge.* —The defendant juſtifies under an execution from a *city court:* The reply is, that the cauſe of action aroſe without the juriſdiction of that court; but this doth not appear from the face of the proceedings, and it is now too late to ſhew it by matter *dehors* the record. The plaintiff in that action might be ignorant of the fact, or the matter in its nature doubtful; and if the de-fendant would ſuffer the proceſs to go on, and not plead the matter in abatement, he ſhould be conſidered as having waved the matter of juriſdiction entirely, and not allowed afterwards to draw it in queſtion by an action of falſe im-priſonment. And ſo was *Truſcott's caſe,* 1. *Ld. Raymond,* 229, in which the former deciſions were brought up, and this point ſettled.

* Ante

SUFFREIN and COLEY *against* PRINDLE.

Diftinction where it is the duty of the defendant to give notice, or the plaintiff to make demand.

THIS action was brought upon the following written promife (viz.) " This balance of 44*l*. 4*s*. is agreed to be paid in good " Weft-India rum, delivered in New-Haven, " as foon as I have any come to hand; or if " none fhould come, to procure it at the cur- " rent market price, and deliver it to *John* " *Suffrein* or *William Coley*, or order. Mr. " *Helmns* or capt. *Sloan* to judge of the quality " and price of the rum."

It was averred in the declaration, that the defendant, on the firft day of January 1783, had good Weft-India rum come to hand, fufficient to pay faid fum, but had not paid it.

The defendant pleaded, that he did not receive any rum until the 10th day of February 1783, and then only forty-nine gallons, which he delivered to the plaintiffs, together with fome other articles, to the amount of 32*l*. 7*s*. which they received in part payment of faid fum of 44*l*. 4*s*.—That the refidue of faid rum did not come to hand before the 15th day of Auguft, 1783, at which time, and at all times fince, he hath ftood ready to deliver faid rum to the plaintiffs, or their order, in New-Haven; and that he could not find the plaintiffs, or any perfon by them authorifed to receive faid rum, to whom he could make legal tender; and that the plaintiffs had never demanded the fame: And concluded by traverfing, that on the firft day of January, 1783, the defendant had good Weft-India rum come to hand fufficient to pay faid debt.

To this there was a demurrer, and judgement for the plaintiffs: For,

BY THE WHOLE COURT.—The plea amounts only to a traverfe of the defendant's having rum

rum come to hand in January, 1783, fufficient to pay the debt, which is an immaterial fact; if his own did not feafonably arrive, he was, by the terms of the contract, to procure other rum: So that the plea is ill, and judgement muft be for the plaintiffs, if the declaration is good: To which only it is objected, that the plaintiffs alledged no demand; but this was not neceffary; they had right of action without any demand, after waiting a reafonable time for the defendant's rum to arrive, or other rum to be procured, and not being notified that it was ready; it was the defendant's duty to give notice, and there was no lien on the plaintiffs to make demand.

BURROWS *against* FITCH.

THIS action was againft the fheriff of New-Haven county, for the neglect of his deputy in not levying and returning an execution which iffued on a judgement of the fuperior court, holden in the county of Fairfield The action was upon the ftatute regulating fheriffs, in which it is enacted, " That if fuch fheriff or " conftable fhall not execute the writ, or fhall " neglect to make return thereof, or fhall make " falfe or undue return; on complaint thereof " made to the court or juftice to which it was " made returnable, the court or juftice may " enquire thereof, by the evidence produced, " and if he be found in default, the court or " juftice may fet a fuitable fine upon him, and " award damages to the party aggrieved."

On demurrer, judgement was for the plaintiff.   And,

P   BY

BY THE WHOLE COURT.—The only exception to the declaration is, that the ſtatute
on which this action is brought requires that
the complaint ſhould be made to the ſame court
that granted the execution on which, &c. and
therefore this action ſhould have been brought
in the county of Fairfield, and not in the
county of New-Haven. The court is of opinion, that this court is the ſame within the
meaning of the ſtatute, ſitting in any county in
the ſtate ; and therefore ſuch action may be
maintained in the county where either party
dwells. The declaration is therefore ſufficient.

WILFORD *and Others againſt* GRANT.

PETER GRANT, and *Eleanor* his wife,
brought their action of treſpaſs againſt
*Joſeph Wilford, Iſaac Smith, John Blackſtone,
2d, Timothy Blackſtone, Noadiah Rogers,* and
Samuel Hoadley, jun. for an aſſault and battery
committed upon ſaid *Eleanor.* At the time of
trial, *Wilford* and the two *Blackſtones* made default. The other defendants appeared and
pleaded the general iſſue, on which the jury
found a verdict for the plaintiffs, and 75*l.* damages ; and judgement was rendered againſt
all the defendants.

The defendants then brought this writ of
error *de recordo quod coram nobis reſidet,* aſſigning the following errors in fact :

1. That *Timothy* and *John Blackſtone* were,
at the time of bringing the ſuit, and at the time
of rendering judgement, minors under the age
of twenty-one years, and totally incapable of
appearing,

1786.

Wilford,
&c.
against
Grant.

appearing, anfwering or defending in faid fuit in any other way than by guardians; and that the plaintiffs did not cite any perfon to appear as guardian to faid minors, nor was any perfon ever appointed by the court.

2. That the court did proceed to render one entire judgement againft all the defendants in faid fuit for entire damages; whereas faid *Timothy* and *John* have never had a day in court, or an opportunity to put in any plea, or to be heard on faid matters; and no damages ought to have been given or affeffed againft them.

The defendant in error pleaded in abatement to the writ; that faid judgement was recovered againft the plaintiffs, in error for a trefpafs committed on faid *Eleanor*, who has fince deceafed, fhe then being wife of the defendant in error; therefore, the prefent defendant cannot be confidered as party or privy to faid action; fo as to be heard on the merits thereof, if faid judgement fhould be reverfed; and that execution hath been taken out on faid judgement, and duly levied on land, and faid lands duly appraifed and fet off.

The plaintiffs in error replied,—That there is not any executor or adminiftrator of the faid *Eleanor* deceafed; but that the faid *Eleanor* left fundry heirs, each of whom are minors under the age of twenty-one years; and that the defendant in error is the father and natural guardian to each and every of the heirs of the faid deceafed, and has been duly fummoned and notified to appear and defend in this cafe.

The replication was adjudged fufficient, and the action ordered to proceed; and then on the plea, *in nullo eft erratum*, judgement was reverfed in part only.

By the whole Court.—The judgement complained of is againft minors and adults, as

　　joint

joint trefpaffers ; minors are prefumed wanting in difcretion to manage their own caufes, or to appoint and inſtruct attornies ; guardians are therefore to be affigned, who fhall take care for them, and be accountable : In this cafe none were affigned, and judgement went againſt the minors by default, through the neglect of the then plaintiff to inform the court of their minority, which he ought to have done before he took judgement againſt them by default or otherwife. But the principal queſtion is, can the judgement be reverfed as to them, and ſtand good againſt the reſt ? No reafon appears *rerum naturâ*, why it ſhould be reverfed as to the adults alfo : They were fairly tried and convicted, and they might have been taken alone at firſt, or the plaintiff might have entered a *nolle profequi* as to the others ; and as this recovery was for a tort, no contribution could have been compelled, if one had been obliged to pay the contents of the execution. If a judgement muſt be reverfed as to all, merely to give relief to one who may be entitled to it, there will be unneceffary expence and delay of juſtice, and in cafes circumſtanced like the prefent, a failure of it : For the right of action being merely perfonal, and the original plaintiff dead, the action cannot be commenced again *de novo*.— The common law rules of England are indeed againſt a reverfal in part only, in a cafe like this, though it is admitted in others without any apparent diverfity of reafon : As if an infant and one of full age join in a fine, there fhall be a reverfal *quoad* the infant only ; fo where judgement is erroneous only with regard to coſts, it may be reverfed as to them, and ſtand good as to the debt or damages ; but it doth not appear that this rule has been adopted in practice here, fo as to become authoritative.

tive. The common law of England we are to
pay great deference to, as being a general fyftem of improved reafon, and a fource from
whence our principles of jurifprudence have
been moftly drawn: The rule, however, which
have not been made our own by adoption, we
are to examine, and fo far vary from them as
they may appear contrary to reafon or unadapt-
ed to our local circumftances, the policy of our
law, or fimplicity of our practice; which, for
the reafons above fuggefted, we do in this cafe,
and reverfe the judgment as to the minors only.

*This judgement was afterwards affirmed in the
fupreme court of errors.*

WILLES *and his Wife against* OLCOTT.

ACTION of diffeifin,—On fpecial plead-ings the cafe was—That. *John Knowles*, by his laft *will*, dated the 30th day of November, 1753, among other things, devifed the lands, in queftion to his " daughter *Mary* " *Knowles*, and the heirs of her body forever." *Mary Knowles* was married in June, 1762, to *Alexander Chalker*, and had iffue a. daughter, *Bridget* (wife of the plaintiff) born September, 1764. The faid *Mary* having heirs born of her body, did alien the lands on the 6th day of June, 1765, by a deed of bargain and fale, executed by herfelf and hufband; and by feveral mefne conveyances it came regularly to the defendant.

On demurrer,—It was contended that this was a limited eftate, and no more than a life eftate in *Mary Knowles;* therefore fhe could not alien the fee, but that it defcended to *Bridget Chalker*, the plaintiff's wife.

On the other fide it was urged, that this devife created a conditional fee, and that the condition was performed when *Mary* had married and had heirs of her body; and that the eftate then vefted in her, as a fee fimple: That the Englifh ftatute of *Weftminfter*, 2d, 13th *Edward* 1. entitled the Statute de donis Conditionalibus, did never extend to this country, and hath never been adopted here; therefore, fuch tenures ought not to be conftrued to be eftates tail in this ftate.

BY THE COURT.—Uniformity of decifion is to be preferved. The point in this cafe hath been twice recently adjudged, in the cafes of *Allen* vs. *Bunce*, and *Devey* vs. *Foot;* and on

the

the following principles: That the intent of the teftator was to be purfued, where it did not interfere with the policy of law: That the intent in the prefent cafe obvioufly was to create an eftate tail, and not a conditional fee. A limitation in tail, fo far as related to the firft donee in tail, might be for very good reafons; and it does not interfere with the policy of law, like perpetuities, or more than any life eftate: And that the late ftatute, admitting limitations in tail, as relative to the firft donee, might well be confidered as in affirmance of the common law. Judgement was therefore for the plaintiffs.

N. B. Judge PITKIN *excufed himfelf from judging in this cafe, being related to one of the parties.*

KIBBE *against* KIBBE.

THIS was an action of debt, on a judgement rendered by the court of common pleas in the county of Berkfhire, and commonwealth of Maffachufetts.

The defendant pleaded in abatement, " That " at the time of bringing the action to the court " of common pleas, upon which the judgement " referred to in the plaintiff's declaration was " rendered, he, the defendant, was an inhabi- " tant of the town of Somers, in the county " of Hartford; and that the plaintiff, in faid " original action, prayed out a certain pretend- " ed writ againft the defendant, in the words " following, *to wit:*

" Berkfhire

Kibbee
againſt
Kibbee.

" Berkſhire, ſſ.

" The commonwealth of Maſſachuſetts,
" To *James Kibbe*, of Somers, in the county
" of Hartford, and ſtate of Connecticut,
" huſbandman, *Greeting* :

" W E command you that you appear at our
" next court of common pleas, to be holden at
" Great-Barrington, within and for our ſaid
" county of Berkſhire, on the third Tueſday
" of November next; then and there to an-
" ſwer unto *Stephen Kibbe*, of Loudon, in the
" county aforeſaid, yeoman, in a plea of co-
" venant broken, which is at large ſet forth in
" the original writ; which plea the ſaid *Stephen*
" hath commenced againſt you, to be heard and
" tried at the ſaid court ; and your goods and
" eſtate are attached, to the value of two hun-
" dred pounds, being for ſecurity to ſatisfy the
" judgement which the ſaid *Stephen* may reco-
" ver upon the aforeſaid trial. Fail not of ap-
" pearance, at your peril. Witneſs, WILLI-
" AM WHITING, Eſq. at Great-Barrington,
" the 28th day of October, in the year of our
" Lord 1784.

" HENRY WMS. DWIGHT, Clerk."

That the plaintiff having prayed out ſaid pretended writ, he cauſed the ſame to be left, or
a copy thereof, at the dwelling-houſe of him,
the defendant, in ſaid Somers, by ſome perſon
unknown to the defendant: That the aforeſaid
writ, or copy thereof, was the only notice or
ſummon ever given or made to the defendant,
to appear and anſwer; and ſaid judgement was
proceeded to, and rendered 'againſt the defendant, upon the ground and authority of ſaid
writ, iſſued and left at the defendant's houſe, in
ſaid Somers, as aforeſaid, and in no other way
or manner whatever.

Whereupon

Whereupon the defendant fays, That he had not legal notice, nor had faid court of common pleas any authority to iffue any procefs againft the defendant, or proceed to render judgement thereon, upon fuch pretended writ, left at the defendant's houfe, in faid Somers, as aforefaid; nor was the defendant holden by law to make any anfwer thereto; and faid judgement is ill founded and void, and no fuit or action can or ought to be maintained thereon; all which the defendant is ready to verify, &c.

The plaintiff *replied*, That he brought his action againft the defendant before faid court of common pleas, in the words following, *to wit:*

" Berkfhire ff.
" Commonwealth of Maffachufetts,
" To the fheriff of our county of Berkfhire,
" his under fheriff or deputy, *Greeting:*
" WE command you to attach the goods or
" eftate of *James Kibbee*, of Somers, in the
" county of Hartford, and ftate of Connecti-
" cut, hufbandman, to the value of 200*l.*—and
" for want thereof take the body of the faid
" *James*, if he may be found in your precinct,
" and him fafely keep, fo that you have him
" before our juftices of our court of common
" pleas, next to be holden at Great-Barring-
" ton, within and for our faid county of Berk-
" fhire, on the third Tuefday of November
" next; then and there in our faid court to an-
" fwer to *Stephen Kibbee*, of Loudon, in our
" faid county, yeoman, in a plea of covenant
" broken; and whereupon the faid *Stephen*
" complains for this *(to wit:)* That whereas the
" faid *James*, at Somers aforefaid *(to wit)* at
" Great-Barrington aforefaid, on the 23d day
" of February, in the year of our Lord, 1763,
" by his deed pole, the date whereof was the

Q

" day

" day and year laft aforefaid; which deed was
" well executed by the faid *James*, fealed with
" his feal, ready in court to be produced, for
" and in confideration of the fum of 64*l.* law-
" ful money, by the faid *Stephen* well and tru-
" ly paid to the faid *James*, did give, grant,
" fell, and confirm to the faid *Stephen*, his heirs
" and affigns forever, a certain piece or lot of
" land, lying and being in Tyringham, in our
" faid county of Berkfhire, containing feventy
" acres, be the fame more or lefs, which was
" laid out on *Samuel Levemore's* right, and is
" number 194, and bounds, &c. Alfo, one
" other tract or lot of land, in faid Tyringham,
" containing fixty-two and an half acres, be
" the fame more or lefs, which was laid out on
" *William White's* right, and is number 142.
" Alfo, a right in place of commonancy, which
" is known by the name of the Equivalent Land.
" Said right did belong to *Samuel Levemore*, a-
" forefaid, and faid lots were not then laid out.
" To have and to hold to the faid *Stephen*, his
" heirs and affigns forever: And the faid *James*
" by his deed aforefaid, did covenant with faid
" *Stephen*, his heirs and affigns, that at and un-
" til the enfealing thereof, he was well feized
" of the premifes, as a good indefeafible eftate
" in fee fimple; and that he had good right
" and lawful authority to bargain and fell the
" fame in manner and form aforefaid; and that
" the fame were free and clear of all incum-
" brances whatever. And furthermore, the
" faid *James* did then and there, by his deed
" aforefaid, covenant with the faid *Stephen*, his
" heirs and affigns, to warrant and defend the
" above granted premifes to him the faid
" *Stephen*, his heirs and affigns, againft all
" claims and demands whatever. And now
" the faid *Stephen* in fact fays, that the land
                          " aforefaid

" aforefaid was under incumbrances, and that
" the faid *James* hath not warranted, fecured
" and defended the abovefaid premifes to him
" the faid *Stephen*; againft all claims and de-
" mands whatever: And the faid *James*, his
" covenants aforefaid hath not kept, but
" broken' to the damage of the faid *Stephen*
" (as he faith) the fum of 200*l.*—which fhall
" then and there be made to appear, with other
" due damages. And have you there this writ,
" with your doings therein. Witnefs, W I L L I-
" A M W H I T I N G, Efq. at Great-Barrington,
" this 28th day of October, in the year of our
" Lord, 1784.

    " H. W. D. Clerk."

Which faid writ was duly ferved on the defendant, by *Solomon Jackfon*, fheriff's deputy
for faid county of Berkfhire, and by him duly
returned to faid court, with his indorfement
thereon, in the words following, viz.————
" Berkfhire ff. October 29, 1784 : Then, by
" virtue of the within writ, I attached a hand-
" kerchief, fhewn to me by the plaintiff's at-
" torney, to be the eftate of the within named
" *James Kibbee*; and have feafonably fent him
" a fummon, for his appearance at the time and
" place within mentioned, as the law directs."
That the faid fheriff's deputy, agreeable to
his faid indorfement, fent to the defendant faid
fummon, mentioned and recited in the defendant's plea, by the hands of *Nathaniel Wood*,
of Loudon, in faid Berkfhire county, and
Afahel Adams, of Suffield, in faid Hartford
county, who left the fame with the defendant,
and duly made oath to the fame before *Elipha-*
let Terry, Efq. Juftice of the Peace for Hartford county, who made a certificate thereof,
in thefe words, viz.————" Hartford county ff.
" Enfield, November 2d. 1784; perfonally ap-

    " peared

" peared *Nathaniel Wood*, of Loudon, in the
" county of Berkſhire, and commonwealth of
" Maſſachuſetts, and *Aſahel Adams*, of Suffield,
" in ſaid Hartford county, and made ſolemn
" oath, that they have this day left a ſummon
" at the dwelling-houſe of *James Kibbee*, of
" Somers, in ſaid Hartford county, for his ap-
" pearance at the court of common pleas, at
" Great-Barrington, in and for the county of
" Berkſhire, in ſaid commonwealth of Maſſa-
" chuſetts, on the third Tueſday of November
" inſtant; then and there to make anſwer to
" *Stephen Kibbee*, of ſaid Loudon, in a plea of
" covenant broken."——Which writ, with the
ſaid deputy ſheriff's indorſement thereon, and
with ſaid certificate made by ſaid *Eliphalet Terry*, Eſq. were duly returned to ſaid court of
common pleas, for ſaid county of Berkſhire,
and ſaid court thereupon proceeded to render
judgement in ſaid action, in the words following, viz.

" Berkſhire ſſ.—At a court of common pleas,
" begun and holden at Great-Barrington, with-
" in and for the county of Berkſhire, on the
" third Tueſday of November, A. D. 1784.

" *Stephen Kibbee*, of Loudon, in the county
" of Berkſhire, yeoman, plaintiff, againſt *James
" Kibbee*, of Somers, in the county of Hartford,
" and ſtate of Connecticut, huſbandman, defen-
" dant, in a plea of covenant broken *(recit-
" ing the ſubſtance of the declaration.)* The ſaid
" *Stephen* appears in court, by his attorney,
" *Thomas Ives*, gentleman; and the ſaid *James*
" is now three times ſolemnly called to come
" into court, but makes default of appear-
" ance here: Whereupon it is adjudged and
" determined by the court, that in this caſe the
" ſaid *Stephen* do recover againſt the ſaid *James*
" the ſum of 147*l.* 3*s.* 9*d.* lawful money, da-
" mages,

1786.

Kibbe
againſt
Kibbe.

" images, and the coſts of ſuit, taxed at 1*l*. 10*s*.
" 9*d*. And hereof the ſaid *Stephen* may have
" his execution."——All which, by the files
and records of ſaid court of common pleas,
ready in court to be ſhewn, appears; and all
which proceedings aforeſaid were conformable
to the laws and cuſtoms of the ſaid commonwealth of Maſſachuſetts.

The defendant *rejoined*, That ſaid writ was
no otherwiſe ſerved than by leaving ſaid copy
or paper, without any indorſement or return
thereon by any one whatever, or any kind of
notice or intimation of attaching any eſtate
whatever, as in his plea is alledged: And
though true it is the ſaid *Jackſon*, deputy ſheriff, made return of his attaching a handker-
chief, ſhewn to him by the plaintiff's attorney
to be the eſtate of the defendant, yet the defendant ſays that he never did in fact attach or
take any of his eſtate whatever; and ſaid return of ſaid officer is altogether falſe and feign-
ed, and calculated by the plaintiff and his attorney merely to procure and obtain the judgement aforeſaid, and of which return and doings
of ſaid deputy ſheriff the defendant never had
the leaſt notice, until the bringing of this action; and the defendant thereupon ſays, that
the proceedings aforeſaid are altogether illegal,
and not conformable to or warranted by the
laws of this ſtate or any other.

And the plaintiff *ſur-rejoined*—That ſaid
paper left with the defendant in ſervice, was a
ſummon, iſſued and ſigned by the clerk of the
ſaid court of common pleas, for ſaid county of
Berkſhire, for the defendant to appear and anſwer unto the ſaid ſuit before ſaid court; which
is the uſual and common notice for appearance,
agreeable to the laws, uſage and cuſtoms of ſaid
commonwealth; and that the ſaid notice, and
evidence

Kibbe
against
Kibbe.

evidence thereof, and the whole of said procefs, was agreable to said laws, ufages and cuftoms.

To this there was a demurrer, and joinder in demurrer; and judgement for the defendant.

BY THE COURT.—It appears by the pleadings, that the defendant was an inhabitant of the ftate of Connecticut, and was not within the jurifdiction of the court of common pleas for the county of Berkfhire, at the time of the pretended fervice of the writ; therefore, the court had no legal jurifdiction of the caufe, and fo no action ought to be admitted on faid judgement: But full credence ought to be given to judgements of the courts in any of the United States, where both parties are within the jurifdiction of fuch courts at the time of commencing the fuit, and are duly ferved with the procefs, and have or might have had a fair trial of the caufe; all which, with the original caufe of action, ought to appear by the plaintiff's declaration in action of debt on fuch judgement.

Judge DYER faid further,—That the original action was upon a covenant real, and locally annexed where the lands lye; and the judgement being by default, this court never could take cognizance of or examine into the juftice of the caufe; therefore, cannot enforce the judgement on which this action is brought.

Note.—Judge ELLSWORTH *excufed himfelf from giving an opinion in this cafe, having formerly been of counfel.*

The two preceding cafes were adjudged the laft term.

HART *againſt* SMITH.

THIS was a general *indebitatus aſſumpſit*, for money had and received.

The caſe, from the pleadings, was this :—— The plaintiff being brigadier-general of a-brigade of militia, and the defendant a colonel under his command, received of the plaintiff the ſum of 1578*l.* in bills of this ſtate, to be applied to public uſe, and to account. On the 4th day of Jan. 1783, the defendant rendered an account of the application of the monies ſo received, and a ſettlement was made by the parties; the plaintiff gave to the defendant an acquittance from all demands on this account, and the defendant delivered to the plaintiff all his vouchers and other papers relative to the matter : That by means of a double charge and miſentry, two miſtakes had happened in the ſettlement, againſt the plaintiff, to the amount of 202*l.* 14*s.* 6*d.*

On demurrer, the queſtion was, whether this general action of indebitatus aſſumpſit, is ſuſtainable after a ſettlement and acquittance.

Judgement was for the defendant.

By LAW, *Chief Juſtice*, DYER, SHERMAN and PITKIN.——The facts conceded by the pleadings, do not ſupport this action.——It appears by the pleadings, that the only money received by the defendant of the plaintiff, was a ſum of ſtate bills, which he received as a public officer, to pay over to the ſoldiers of his regiment, for which he was accountable ; and if he had failed of performing his undertaking, the plaintiff's legal and proper remedy would have been an action of account : But the defendant having rendered his account to the plaintiff, to his acceptance, and the ſame having

' ing